ALSO IN THE BLASTA BOOKS SERIES

Blasta Books #1: Tacos

Blasta Books #2: Hot Fat

Blasta Books #3: The United Nations of Cookies

Blasta Books #4: Wok

Blasta Books #5: Soup

Blasta Books #6: Tapas

Blasta Books #7: Wasted

Blasta Books #8: Masarap

Blasta Books #9: Funky

Blasta Books #10: Whole Catch

Blasta Books #11: Agak-Agak

Blasta Books #12: Socafro

Blasta Books #13: Larder

Blasta Books #14: Tango

Blasta Books #15: Jibrin

blastabooks.com

MESSY

Text by Aoife McElwain

Illustrated by Ciara Coogan

CONTENTS

Introduction 1

CAN'T COPE
Messy essay: Rest the dough, rest yourself 4
Messy eggs 6
Toast with notions 8
Pimped-up instant noodle pot 10
Can't cope one-pot pasta 12
Hot chocolate with Tunnock's Tea Cake 13

COMFORT FOOD
Messy essay: The worst dinner guests ever 14
Caraway brown bread 18
Seedy loaf 19
Eggs, pickles & Marmite 21
Green eggs 22
Caesar salad 23
Macaroni & cheese 24

BROTH IS A LOVE LANGUAGE
Messy essay: Using your head, heart and gut to say no 26
All-rounder roast chicken 28
Homemade chicken stock 29
Lemon & orzo soup 30
Miso & mushroom broth 32
Spicy coconut noodle soup 33

CRAIC IN THE KITCHEN (AKA PARTY FOOD)

Messy essay: Priority pizza pie 34
Starter: Smoked mackerel bites with beetroot dip 38
Main course: Slow-cooked beef & harissa stew 40
Main course: Queen Cauliflower 42
Sides: Buttered greens 43
Sides: Tahini sauce 44
Sides: Smushed spuds 45
Dessert: Nonchalant meringues 46
Cheese course: Biscuits for cheese 47
Cheese course: An easy cheeseboard 48

LIVING YOUR BEST LIFE IN THE GREAT OUTDOORS

Messy essay: Your best is good enough 50
Peanut butter & chocolate-dipped dates 54
Malty muesli bars 55
Campfire stew 56

LIFE IS SWEET & MESSY

Messy essay: How to fail with good taste 58
Coffee & orange cake 60
Pineapple upside-down cake 62
Pauline's pavlova 64

Index 66

INTRODUCTION

SIMPLE RECIPES FOR CHAOTIC COOKS

Hi. My name is Aoife and I'm a messy cook.

This book is for the distracted bakers and forgetful fermenters, the burners of toast and over-cookers of eggs, and for all the cooks who have scorched countless saucepan bottoms and who know only too well the deflating disappointment of a cake that has failed to rise.

It's for the gloriously messy and chaotically creative kind of folks who leave their house late for a meeting only to realise they're holding a kitchen utensil instead of their phone, then realise that the meeting they're rushing to is happening tomorrow. It's for the folks whose intentions are good – so good – but whose wandering attention and blind commitment to multitasking lead to mishaps and misadventures inside and outside the kitchen.

We, too, can cook.

I should know, because I am one of those chaotic cooks. Alas, many slices of toast have been lost under my watch. Eggs so over-scrambled and rubbery that the hen deserves a formal written apology. One of my greatest achievements in the kitchen is baking cakes that are somehow both burned and under-cooked.

As I've gone from a beginner to a novice to a confident and intuitive cook, I've been struck by how food and cooking offer us so many helpful metaphors for how to live well. Through cooking, eating and sharing, food has given me an outlet to learn and understand how to lasso and wrangle the creativity and drive that are the sunny side of a life lived chaotically. To find a calming, steadying order that creates an even better environment for enjoying the process and being fully present with joy.

So take my hand and let's learn how to cook, messily, together.

WHY AM I SO MESSY?

The story of my life through food took an early turn towards new flavours when my family moved from County Monaghan, on the border of Northern Ireland, to Jeddah, Saudi Arabia, on the coast of the Red Sea, in 1985, when I was three years old. My parents are teachers, and they left the stony grey soil for the sandy brown desert on a two-year career break and stayed for nearly 20 years.

Living in Jeddah meant we had access to falafel, shawarma and hummus long before chickpeas were common on Irish supermarket shelves. We also lived in a multicultural environment, going to an American International School and living in an expat compound, where a typical community party spread could include platters of spring rolls, manakish, adobo, maftoul and biryani alongside tacos, Fruit Roll-Ups and chocolate chip cookies.

Despite this smorgasbord, it was my Nanny Brigid's homegrown Irish spuds dripping in Champion butter that my siblings and I spent our school year in the desert daydreaming about. Nanny B's rhubarb tart is legendary, and I have inherited her penchant for coffee cake. As a child I loved connecting with her through food, and I still connect with her today by making food she loved and taught me to love too.

I figured out early on that food is a way to connect with people I love, but I didn't start learning how to cook until well into my twenties. I was more interested in music as a teenager, plus I had a self-limiting belief that cooking was something that I would never do as well as my Nanny B and my mum did, so why bother trying?

When I was 18, I went to university in London and worked in The Walpole, which was a caff by day and bistro by night with a fierce commitment to truly great ingredients. The wife-and-husband team at The Walpole, Wendy and Louis, spotted my budding curiosity around food and cooking and nourished it wholeheartedly.

I started a food blog in 2009 to learn how to cook, called *I Can Has Cook* in honour of an iconic cat meme of that era. I had high expectations and very little experience apart from a healthy appetite that I indulged often. To my genuine surprise, the blog led to food columns in actual newspapers, writing recipes and restaurant reviews, and I discovered I had a bit of a flair for food styling. That led to more work across print, video and TV, and to more opportunities for learning on the trot.

It was also a time filled with imposter syndrome and toxic perfectionism fuelled by my inner critic, who never missed an opportunity to tell me that I didn't know anything about food or cooking, and who the hell did I think I was to write about it, cook it, take photos of it, video it or talk about it? Fun times.

Part of my imposter syndrome attached itself to my lack of formal training as well as my late start in the kitchen. Looking back, I can see that my approach to learning was to be curious, to listen and to try, and for a home cook, that's more than good enough.

Though I'm mindful not to over-define myself by these four letters (because they make up just one part of who I am), being diagnosed with ADHD in 2020 has been a helpful way to identify the strengths that I might attribute to the diagnosis – creativity, fearlessness, hyperfocus – and to identify the cause of some of my recurring challenges in life, namely, impulsivity, time-blindness and burnout.

The biggest impact of this diagnosis is that it's been a way to dismantle the shame I've carried for a long time around things like having a messy pantry; of always being behind schedule; of not understanding numbers – like, *really* not understanding them; of having Big Feelings; or of suffering extreme bouts of cyclical burnout. For not being able to do things that seemed, bafflingly, to be so easy for others.

I can clearly remember what it feels like not to know how to cook. I remember not understanding what it means 'to brown' meat in a recipe. I vividly remember my first attempt at making pastry in an effort to emulate Nanny B's rhubarb tart; it was a cruel introduction to the phenomenon known as Hot Hands.

Practice has not made me perfect, because perfect doesn't exist. And perfection shouldn't be the goal for home cooking. If we focus on perfection, we may miss out on opportunities for connection – connection with ourselves, with our food and with others – and connection is a key ingredient for joy.

My greatest teachers have been my friends (namely Charlotte, Jocelyn, Cliodhna, Lydia and Zoe) who have shared their love of food and their intuitive cooking with me. Then there are the loved ones who have allowed me to cook for them even when the results were not guaranteed, such as Nialler, Alan and Emma. Every budding cook needs a refined palate nearby.

WHAT DOES THAT ALL HAVE TO DO WITH THIS BOOK?

I trained as a life and career coach in 2020, and I've incorporated some of my favourite coaching tools in this cookbook to help maximise your confidence, creativity and craic in the kitchen. This book is about setting you up to learn, and practise daily, how to fill your own cup through food and cooking without being dragged down by toxic perfectionism or getting swept up in the cult of busyness.

With the right ingredients – a combination of the right tools, a bit of knowledge and some gentle, encouraging support, either from someone who can show you the way or from yourself – and a bit of structure, you'll see that messiness can marinate into joy.

BLASTA BOOKS #16

CAN'T COPE

REST THE DOUGH, REST YOURSELF

What's a common element that ties baking, fermentation and great coffee together?

After the dough is kneaded, it needs to rest until you knock it back. After you've added your gochugaru, the cabbage needs time to sit there and ferment to transform into kimchi. When you brew your coffee, a percolation process ensures the best cup, a quality that instant coffee can never match.

The common thread? Rest.

Taking time to let ingredients do their thing is a respected, time-honoured element of good food and great cooking.

Yet we tend not to apply this same logic to ourselves. Equating our value with what we produce or make or do is more our style. The sanctity of The Product is relentlessly reinforced through human systems like capitalism and consumerism. We're locked in a punishing cycle where we confuse value, merit and worth with money and praise, and how much of them we can get. It's no wonder we have a hard time giving ourselves a break.

I wrote a book about burnout called *Slow at Work*, published in 2018. In it, I interviewed over 60 busy people from around the world about the elusive balance of living up to our potential without feeling exhausted all the time.

An interview that changed my life was with Olympic hurdler Derval O'Rourke. She had retired from athletics and pivoted into the tech start-up world, and she was shocked by how the corporate culture had zero respect for recovery time.

As an athlete, she could divide her work into three clear areas: training, performance and recovery, aka rest. She knew that to maintain a high performance over a long period of time, recovery was an essential part of her job. Her coaches built recovery time into her training sessions, and it was non-negotiable.

This idea that recovery is a part of our job resonated deeply with me. It was like someone was finally giving me permission to rest.

Without rest, we can't function properly in work or in life. Without rest, we're stuck in fight-or-flight mode, compulsively doing, and it leads to one place time and time again: burnout.

Rest is now on my to-do list every day. It takes some effort to rewire inbuilt beliefs that resting makes me lazy, that if I don't produce, I'm not valuable. Writing it on my to-do list helps me to prioritise it and to make sure I don't forget it, undermine its importance or allow work and production to interrupt it.

If you feel like you can't cope, this is a red flag with an antidote: rest. Rest can feel like just another impossible task that you are failing at. I have to finish my work, I have to look after the kids, I have to fix that shelf that has been broken for three years, etc. There is always something to be done. Our work is never finished, so we must seize rest. If you are struggling to prioritise it, ask for help to get the rest you need and deserve.

THE RECIPES

Imagine this: you're in the pit of despair, too exhausted to even board the struggle bus. The idea of cooking for yourself, or even chopping an onion, is far beyond what you have the bandwidth for. You may as well be asking yourself to run a marathon with no training and the wrong shoes.

I know this place. I have been there many times and I will see it again. This section is about how I have learned to cook myself out of burnout.

One of the kindest things you can do for yourself when you're feeling energised and full of joie de vivre is to plan for the inevitable time in the future when you won't be feeling so hot.

Having a well-stocked larder means you have the tools you need to care for yourself when life gets you down, you're in an energy slump, your period is on the way, your family is driving you insane or you've overdone it with your hyperfocus on your latest hobby.

Nobody knows your body better than you. Listen to what your body tells you when you eat certain foods. What brings you comfort? What makes you feel better than you did before you took your first bite?

For me, food is foundational to self-care and fundamental to well-being. I'm not talking about mise en place or deglazing pans or even chopping onions. I'm talking about helping yourself when the chips are down to access even a touch of nutrition and, crucially, to build your own confidence in your ability to look after yourself by making yourself something nice to eat.

When you're burned out, you can be so disconnected from yourself that even the senses of touch, sight, smell and taste can be dulled. Food gives you access to those pleasures. Focus on peeling the garlic cloves and crushing them with a knife. Gently cook the garlic in butter. Pay attention to how the butter looks when it's bubbling in the pan. Smell the garlic frying. This won't solve all your problems (garlic is good, but it's not *that* good), but it may help you to reconnect with the moment you're in. If food is one of your love languages, it may even lift your spirits enough to take the next step back towards yourself.

So let's take our first little step together. Let's scramble some eggs.

MESSY EGGS

SERVES 1

My sister Niamh makes the best scrambled eggs, which is very on brand for her – she is, after all, one of the best people I know. Meanwhile, my scrambled eggs were more rubbery than scrambled; they were always overdone and had that weird, spongy texture of a sad, sad scrambled egg. If you know, you know.

I couldn't figure out what Niamh was doing to achieve such a different result from me until one day, as I watched her preparing her super-special eggs, it finally dawned on me: she wasn't multitasking while scrambling.

Multitasking is a myth, and one that the patriarchy finds delicious. We spend so much of our time juggling tasks in real life and in our brains that we often miss out on the moment.

These messy eggs are scrambled in the pan instead of in a bowl, inspired by the way they make them at my favourite café, The Fumbally. It's not about being perfect, it's about being present.

bread for toast

lots of butter

coffee or tea for drinking

2 eggs

sea salt and freshly ground black pepper

your favourite chilli oil or hot sauce

Make your hot buttered toast.

Make your coffee or tea.

Melt about a tablespoon of butter in a frying pan on a medium-high heat. It's showtime for the eggs now. Give them 100% of your attention for the next few steps, which is approximately 90 seconds in real time. Ready?

When the butter is melted and sizzling, crack the eggs directly into the pan. Use a wooden spoon to immediately start mixing the eggs around, breaking up the whites and yolks. Mix continuously for 15–20 seconds. Let the eggs rest in the pan for 10–15 seconds, then mix again for 15 seconds.

At the 45-second to 1-minute mark, the eggs will be starting to come together. Just watch them for 15 seconds. Don't be tempted to look at your phone or take out the bins or tidy up. Just watch the eggs. That's your one job. Stir them from time to time. My messy eggs are done after 90 seconds. You might want them a little less cooked or a little more cooked.

Serve on top of your buttered toast with a sprinkling of salt and pepper and a generous drizzle of your favourite chilli oil or hot sauce. Best eaten straight away.

MESSY

TOAST WITH NOTIONS

SERVES 1

Sure, you can just grab a slice of toast and slather a bit of hummus on it. No shame in that. But what if you took the time to add a little sprinkle of this and a little squeeze of that to really let yourself know that you're worth it? What's wonderful about toast with notions is you can fill your pantry with goodies with a long shelf life to make this an easily accomplished feat. Improvise with your favourite flavours and with whatever is in your fridge today.

The ideal slice of toast with notions brings colour, taste, smell and texture to your plate. The level of notions in your toast depends on the quality of its foundations, i.e. the bread you're using. Support your local bakery and breadmaker by using the best, yummiest, realest bread you can get your hands on.

COTTAGE CHEESE & BEETROOT

1 tbsp cottage cheese

1 slice of toast

1 small pickled beetroot, sliced

a little lemon zest

sea salt and freshly ground black pepper

a few chopped walnuts

good-quality balsamic vinegar

fresh dill or mint (optional)

HUMMUS & KIMCHI

1 egg

1 tbsp hummus

1 slice of toast

sea salt and freshly ground black pepper

1 tbsp kimchi

1 tbsp shop-bought crispy fried onions

PEANUT BUTTER, BANANA & CACAO NIBS

1 tbsp peanut butter

1 slice of toast

½ banana or apple, thinly sliced

1 tbsp cacao nibs

1 tsp runny honey

For the cottage cheese and beetroot toast, spread the cottage cheese on top of your toast, then arrange the sliced beetroot on the cheese. Use a Microplane grater or zester to add a little lemon zest. Season with salt and pepper, drizzle with balsamic vinegar and top with chopped walnuts and fresh dill or mint if you have it.

For the hummus and kimchi toast, I like a jammy soft-boiled egg, which I achieve by putting a pan of water on the boil, adding the egg and boiling for 6 minutes, then immediately putting the egg in a bowl of cold water to stop it cooking any further. Spread the hummus on top of your toast. Peel and slice the egg and arrange it on top of the hummus. Add a pinch of salt and pepper, then a tablespoon of kimchi. Top with crispy fried onions and never look back.

For the toast with peanut butter, banana and cacao nibs, spread the peanut butter on your toast, then arrange the slices of banana or apple on top. Finish with the cacao nibs and honey.

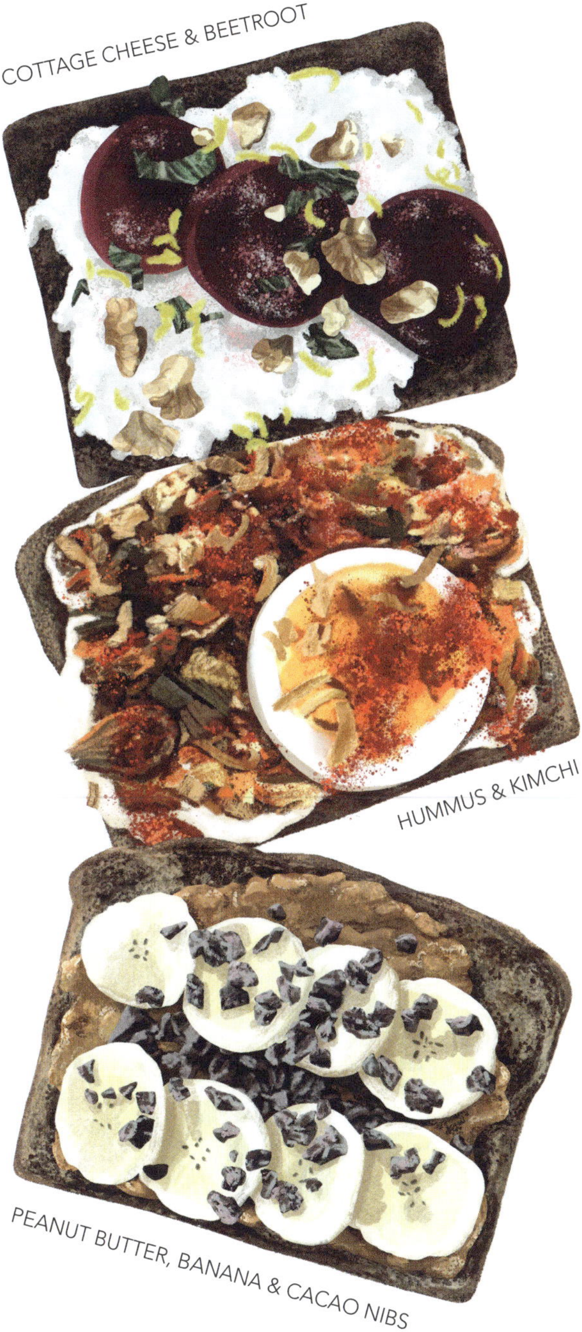

MESSY

COTTAGE CHEESE & BEETROOT

HUMMUS & KIMCHI

PEANUT BUTTER, BANANA & CACAO NIBS

OTHER IDEAS FOR TOAST WITH NOTIONS

Fish fingers and grilled tomatoes

Basil and balsamic tomatoes

Figs, ricotta, thyme and honey

Ham, cheese and cornichons

Pear, blue cheese and walnuts

Smoked mackerel and pickled radish

See *Blasta Books #13: Larder* for even more toast ideas.

PIMPED-UP INSTANT NOODLE POT

SERVES 1

Some days are sent from the depths to test us. On those days, I like to crawl back into bed by noon with a pimped-up instant noodle pot. I like the Koka brand, which is widely available, but you can get the best instant noodles that come in all shapes and sizes in Asian food stores. I add some fresh ingredients and a few pantry staples, like frozen dumplings, to bog-standard instant noodles. It's not gourmet but it's certainly a step up from cereal for supper.

shop-bought frozen dumplings (optional)

1 instant noodle pot

1 tsp miso or doenjang (optional)

a small handful of kale, finely chopped

1 tbsp frozen peas, defrosted in a bit of hot water

1 tsp teriyaki sauce

1 tbsp chilli oil

I like to have dumplings in my freezer for emergencies, and specifically for pimping up instant noodles. If using, just follow the packet instructions for steaming them or cooking them from frozen.

Follow the instructions on your instant noodle pot. You can stir in the miso or doenjang to bulk up the stock if you like.

When your noodles are ready, add the cooked dumplings (if using), chopped kale, peas and teriyaki sauce to your pot. Top with a drizzle of chilli oil and take it back to bed.

MESSY

CAN'T COPE ONE-POT PASTA

SERVES 1 WITH LOTS OF LEFTOVERS

This recipe is for those times when you truly cannot cope – when the idea of chopping an onion may as well be climbing a mountain. This is a base sauce that you can master and build upon – when you're ready, add some slow-cooked onions and garlic for a deeper, yummier, better flavour.

Cooking the pasta in the same pot means less washing up. You can also cook the pasta separately, then use any leftover sauce with eggs on toast for breakfast or lunch the next day.

1 tbsp olive oil

1 tbsp smoked paprika

1 tsp garlic powder

1 x 400g (14oz) tin of chopped tomatoes

juice of ½ lemon

1 tbsp sugar (brown is best)

sea salt and freshly ground black pepper

200g (7oz) macaroni, penne or rigatoni

400ml (1²/₃ cups) water

TO SERVE:
freshly grated Parmesan cheese

fresh basil, if you have it

Heat the olive oil in a sauté pan or a saucepan on a medium heat. Add the smoked paprika and garlic powder and cook for just 1 minute, then stir in the tomatoes, lemon juice, sugar and a generous pinch of salt and pepper. Add the pasta and water and stir well.

Simmer on a medium heat, uncovered, for 20–25 minutes, stirring from time to time so the pasta doesn't stick to the bottom of the pan. The sauce will have thickened and look a bit glossy and the pasta will be cooked through. Add a little more water if needed, but the pasta should be nicely al dente after 20–25 minutes.

Serve with loads of freshly grated Parmesan cheese and some torn fresh basil or whatever fresh herbs you have.

HOT CHOCOLATE WITH TUNNOCK'S TEA CAKE

SERVES 1

Putting a Tunnock's Tea Cake into my hot chocolate is one of my proudest creative achievements. Am I a hero? I really can't say … but yes. Yes, I am.

240ml (1 cup) whole milk or plant-based alternative (oat milk works well)

1 heaped tbsp cacao powder

1 heaped tbsp sugar (ideally brown sugar)

a pinch of ground cinnamon

a pinch of ground ginger

a pinch of chilli flakes

1 Tunnock's Tea Cake

Put the milk, cacao powder, sugar, cinnamon, ginger and chilli flakes in a saucepan and bring to a gentle simmer, using a whisk to blend the powder into the milk. Simmer gently for about 5 minutes so the flavours get time to mingle. Don't let the milk boil or it will overflow and make a big mess.

Prepare your tea cake by using a sharp knife to separate the chocolate-covered marshmallow dome from the biscuit base.

Pour your hot chocolate into your favourite mug. Add the marshmallow dome on top and serve the biscuit base on the side for dunking. You're welcome.

COMFORT FOOD

THE WORST DINNER GUESTS EVER

Picture this. You're throwing a dinner party and two of the worst dinner guests imaginable show up. Let's call them Petunia and Aunt Linda.

The first offence is that they arrive way earlier than all the other guests. In fact, they show up immediately after you send your invites.

'Do you think you should remodel the room before the party?' Petunia asks. 'It just isn't *quite* right.'

'That's a start, but your whole house isn't good enough,' Aunt Linda chimes in. 'What if your friends decide they don't want to be your friends when they see how disorganised your kitchen is? And, oh, you're going to cook that recipe? Mmm'kay,' she adds, raising a fault-finding eyebrow, while Petunia begins to panic.

'Well, maybe if we control everything so that it's completely and utterly perfect,' says Petunia, tight-lipped with intensity, 'like, everything, down to the silverware and the table setting and the ingredients and the background music and the conversation that you will practise beforehand into your mirror, then maybe, just *maybe* they'll still want to be your friends.'

'Yeah. That'll never work,' says Aunt Linda.

And … scene.

Sound familiar? If so, then you, like me, might have a touch of perfectionism and her best friend, the inner critical voice, two toxic tenants that live inside most of our heads. It's messy in there.

If I could change one thing for my younger self – if I could lighten her load and help her to skip to the end – I wish I could turn off her tendency for perfectionism.

Part of the reason I stayed trapped in the clutches of this toxic mindset for so long was because I didn't even realise I was a perfectionist because I've never done anything perfectly in my entire life.

Do you know who loves toxic perfectionism? Inner critics. Because clinging on to the myth of perfectionism means you will never succeed. Ever.

Despite having a loving family and a life overflowing with privilege, I've had a painfully loud inner critical voice for as long as I can remember. I can sort of make light of it now, but it's painful to be trapped with a bully 24/7. The real kicker about this kind of negative self-attack is that your body doesn't know that thoughts aren't real. Your body goes into fight-or-flight mode when it's being attacked, even if it's just your inner critic attacking you.

In a moment of transformative guidance, my therapist suggested that I give my inner critic a name to try to separate the voice from myself, to externalise it and help me to notice when it showed up. To lessen the feeling of an inner self-attack by understanding what had triggered it and how to move past it.

If you've read my book *Slow at Work*, you'll have already met my inner critic, Aunt Linda. She isn't named after my real-life aunties, who are all lovely. She's named after a classic Kristen Wiig character from *Saturday Night Live*, a grumpy older lady who does film reviews but finds fault in everything so fervently as to make it laughable. This was the perfect character for me to associate my inner critical voice with.

If comparison is the thief of joy, then perfectionism is an aiding and abetting accomplice. When we are working from a place of comparison – whether we're comparing ourselves to a real person, e.g. Nigella, or an imaginary person, aka Them – we tend to be cut off or distracted from using our own voice. We can slip into copying others – not in a healthy, aspirational way, but in a way that sets us up for failure and has us living inauthentically to ourselves.

What I know to be true is this: only you can do what you do, if you do it with full confidence in your own head, heart, gut and soul, or whatever you want to call your most full and complete self. I believe this is true in life, and it's definitely true in the kitchen.

It's kind of like how you and I could both have the same recipe for sourdough or a homemade cheese or kimchi. We could follow the exact same steps using identical ingredients. But because I am making it in my kitchen, with its unique ecosystem and temperature and humidity, with my own hands and with the experience I've had in my life leading up to this moment, it's almost guaranteed that my bread or cheese or kimchi will taste remarkably different to yours.

It's the same for any expression of our creativity or our energy. We put our own ingredients in and we get our own unique expression out, and if we're not wasting energy thinking about what other people might do or how they might express themselves, then we have so much more energy to funnel into our own expression.

When I first gave her a name, I thought I could get rid of Aunt Linda for good. If I did self-care and mental health well enough – if I was perfect at looking after myself – she would leave. I would have no need for her.

Ten years later, I'm still working alongside Aunt Linda in almost everything I do, but my relationship with her is much softer than it was a decade ago. She's still a bitch, but these days I'm more prepared because I know when she's likely to show up and how to talk her off the ledge. My girlfriend, Anstice, knows when she's in the room. My friends, family and close colleagues know her by name. She's sneaky, so if I don't realise she's taken the reins, my loved ones can give me a nudge to shake off the Aunt Linda vibes.

She was with me for the whole process of writing this book, as I knew she would be. I was ready for her. Overall, we've worked together pretty well on this project, but at times I had to take her aside for a little chat and tell her that she was being a bit of a silly billy and that her fears of my forced exile from humanity if people don't like my recipes because they're not as good as Darinajuliajamie's will probably not come to pass.

Realising that self-care is a practice that some days we will nail and some days we will fail is another little layer of the onion of self-care. It's not a process with a beginning, middle and end. There is no end goal where we are Our Best Selves every second of every day. Instead, we can practise being kind to ourselves like we practise baking our favourite cake, learning a language or playing the ukulele. Being a good pal to yourself takes practice. Self-care is messy, and don't let anyone tell you otherwise.

THE RECIPES

Food is complicated for many people, for many reasons. It's not joyful or comforting for everyone.

I've had battles with my weight and my body image. I've been overweight and underweight. I came of age in the 1990s and early aughts, how could I not come out unscathed? It takes a lot of work to rewrite the hardwiring that your value is connected to how you look in a pair of jeans.

I still have bouts of disordered eating, where my toxic perfectionism tries to control food and its impact on my weight to feel better about myself. I can overeat to the point of stomach-ache, to dull an intolerable feeling of sadness or pain or upset.

I have always comforted myself through food, and it's a coping mechanism that I have learned to trust. I try to stay connected to my body by paying attention to how I feel. My body changes when I'm sad and it changes when I'm happy. I trust myself to manage those changes. I haven't owned a weighing scale for over a decade.

I know when my body is seeking comfort through food and, within reason, I let her do her thing. Knowledge is knowing when a bowl of Coco Pops is exactly what the doctor ordered, and wisdom is knowing when not to have a third bowl.

Real comfort food, to me, is real food. When I need a hug in food form, give me eggs, greens and cheese. Granted, greens may not be everyone's idea of comfort food. But I've listened to my body when she has told me that greens – like kale and, my favourite, cavolo nero – make me feel so much better for having eaten them, and they're so easy to cook.

CARAWAY BROWN BREAD

MAKES 1 MEDIUM LOAF

My girlfriend Anstice is the butter to my bread and the loaf of my life. She has been perfecting her brown soda bread recipe, a version of Darina Allen's, since she moved from London to Connemara a few years ago. I love how each loaf is a little different. Not all loaves are created equal – while practice doesn't make perfect, some loaves really are better than others, just like our days in this life. I get such comfort from knowing we're never very far away from a freshly baked loaf of brown bread in our house.

300g (2 cups) wholemeal flour

200g (1¾ cups) plain flour

a handful of porridge oats

1 tbsp caraway seeds

1 tsp baking soda

½ tsp sea salt

500–700ml (approx. 2–3 cups) buttermilk

Preheat your oven to 180°C fan (350°F fan). Dust a baking tray with a little flour.

Put all the dry ingredients in a big bowl and mix using a wooden spoon, then make a well in the centre and pour in three-quarters of the buttermilk. Mix with the wooden spoon until it comes together into a shaggy dough, adding more buttermilk if it needs it. Bring the dough together with your hands, but don't knead the bread – the more you handle brown bread, the tougher it'll be. The dough should hold its shape while still feeling squishy.

Sprinkle some flour on your clean kitchen counter or table, then turn the ball of dough out onto it and shape it into a round or oblong, flat-ish loaf shape by hand, again being careful not to overwork the bread.

Now put it on the flour-dusted baking tray. Cut a cross in the top to let the fairies out and pop it in the preheated oven. Bake for 40 minutes, then check it by tapping the bottom: if it sounds hollow, it should be cooked. If it doesn't sound hollow, flip it over and put it back in the oven for 10 minutes.

Take the bread out of the oven and wrap it in a clean tea towel – this will keep the crust a little soft. Let it cool before cutting into slices and eating.

SEEDY LOAF

MAKES 1 SMALL LOAF

At a time when Anstice had banished carbs from her diet (we are women of the 1980s – we were raised to think of carbs as the enemy), her Danish friend shared this culinary life raft of a recipe for a seeded loaf. It's marvellous with cheese, smoked fish, pickled vegetables and any Scandi-adjacent treats.

It's also a very forgiving recipe. If you stick with the measurements below, you can use whatever seeds and nuts you have. Anstice loves caraway seeds, but you can replace them with fennel or poppy seeds. I love this loaf with the eggs, pickles and Marmite on page 21.

250g (1½ cups) mixed seeds (sunflower, pumpkin, golden linseeds, hemp, etc.)

50g (½ cup) walnuts

50g (⅓ cup) hazelnuts

50g (½ cup) almonds

2 tsp caraway, fennel or poppy seeds

½ tsp sea salt

2 eggs

Preheat the oven to 180°C fan (350°F). Line a small loaf tin (14.5cm x 8.25cm (5¾in x 3¼in)) with non-stick baking paper, making sure plenty of paper is left hanging over the sides of the tin. This is because the mixture is very wet and you don't want it to spill out.

Put the mixed seeds, nuts, caraway, fennel or poppy seeds and salt in a large bowl and mix to combine. Crack in the eggs and mix again until the mixture is quite wet, as opposed to sticky like a dough.

Pour the mixture into the lined loaf tin. Bake in the preheated oven for 40 minutes, until lightly browned and hardened into a solid loaf.

Allow the loaf to cool completely in the tin before using the paper to lift it out onto a wire rack. Peel away the paper and slice as you go. Store it in an airtight container at room temperature for up to a week. It's a hardy little loaf so it's a great one to bring on beach picnics, but it's also so good toasted.

EGGS, PICKLES & MARMITE

SERVES 2

This simple plate of comfort was gifted to me by Anstice's great friends Lara and Henry. Henry served this to family and friends one morning on a beach in Connemara. Sounds idyllic, right? It was actually freezing and starting to rain. My gas hob ran out of gas halfway through boiling the eggs, so we all had to run inside and finish our picnic indoors. It was a perfectly imperfect picnic. Now, whenever I taste this dish, I feel the messy comfort of that gathering. The salt of the pickles and Marmite combined with the egg and cheese hit all the right flavour notes, and it's great at any time of day. The addition of Marmite is, of course, optional depending on whether you love it or loathe it.

2 eggs

2 slices of bread, for toasting

butter

Marmite

Cheddar cheese

1 gherkin or pickle, finely diced

sea salt and freshly ground black pepper

A hard-boiled egg is best for this. Put your eggs in a pot of cold water and bring to a boil, then turn down the heat and simmer for 8–10 minutes for a slightly jammy hard-boiled egg. Using a slotted spoon, transfer the eggs to a bowl of cold water to stop them cooking any further. Once they're cool, you can peel them and slice them into rounds.

Toast your slices of bread and top with plenty of butter and as much Marmite as you dare.

Slice your Cheddar so you have enough to cover your toast – two to four slices depending on the size of your bread – then top your toast and cheese with your sliced hard-boiled eggs.

Scatter the diced gherkin or pickle over the top. Add a bit of salt, especially if you're not using Marmite, and some black pepper. Serve with a mug of tea.

GREEN EGGS

SERVES 2–4

Green eggs are a fabulous vehicle for all kinds of greens. I've used leeks and spinach here, but the same amount of kale, chard or cabbage works well too. Anstice grows our spinach, and its lovely, wide leaves make it less wilty and watery than the shop-bought kind (and yes, I do feel rather smug about it). I love making this dish in spring, especially when the three-cornered leeks or wild garlic are growing in their usual spots. This can be easily doubled to serve to a larger crowd, provided you have a pan that's big enough.

a knob of butter, for frying

2 large leeks, thinly sliced

4 garlic cloves, peeled but left whole and crushed

1 tsp cumin seeds

2 large handfuls of spinach, roughly chopped

a handful of three-cornered leeks, wild garlic or 1 spring onion, thinly sliced

sea salt and freshly ground black pepper

4 eggs

FOR THE DRESSING:

2 heaped tbsp natural yogurt

1 heaped tbsp tahini

1 tbsp lemon juice

TO SERVE:

chilli oil (optional)

three-cornered leek flowers, fresh mint or parsley (optional)

toasted sourdough

a squeeze of lemon

Melt a generous knob of butter in a large non-stick frying pan on a medium-high heat. When the butter is starting to foam, add the leeks and the whole crushed garlic cloves to the pan. Fry happily, not furiously, for about 10 minutes, stirring occasionally, until the leeks are lovely and soft.

Stir in the cumin seeds and fry for 1 minute. Add the spinach and the three-cornered leeks or spring onion (or whatever greens you're using). Cook for a couple of minutes, until the greens have wilted. Season with salt and pepper.

Make four wells in the greens. Crack an egg into each one, then cover the pan with its lid (a large heatproof plate will also work if you don't have a lid). Cook for 8–12 minutes, until the eggs are cooked through but ideally still a bit runny.

Make your dressing by mixing the yogurt, tahini and lemon juice together. Add a little water, a teaspoon at a time, to thin the sauce to a runny, drizzling consistency.

Sprinkle a little more salt and pepper on top of the eggs and greens, then add a drizzle of chilli oil (if using) and top with the yogurt dressing. A final flourish of three-cornered leek flowers or a bit of fresh mint or parsley would be delightful, but only if you have them to hand. Serve the whole pot straight to the table so everyone can dig in, with plenty of toasted sourdough bread on the side. Add a little extra squeeze of lemon juice at the last minute – it really brightens up the flavours.

CAESAR SALAD

SERVES 2

A Caesar salad is a joyful gateway from sandwich to salad. This is an easy little homemade Caesar-style dressing. You could make it even yummier by making your own mayonnaise, but I always have a shop-bought Caesar dressing in the fridge for emergencies.

2 Baby Gems or 1 romaine lettuce, roughly chopped

a large handful of croutons, shop-bought or homemade

cooked shredded chicken, if you have it and want to make this a chicken Caesar salad (see page 28)

cooked bacon lardons (optional)

FOR THE DRESSING:

2 anchovies in oil

1 garlic clove

a large handful of finely grated Parmesan, plus extra for the salad

juice of ½ lemon

4 tbsp mayonnaise

2 tbsp Worcestershire sauce

sea salt and freshly ground black pepper

To make the dressing, put the anchovies and garlic on a chopping board and chop them finely until you have a smooth paste (or you can use a pestle and mortar). Transfer to a bowl and stir in the Parmesan, lemon juice, mayonnaise and Worcestershire sauce. Add salt and pepper to taste.

Get your salad together by putting the lettuce in a large serving bowl. Add half of the dressing and toss to coat. Scatter over your croutons and a bit more finely grated or shaved Parmesan. Add some cooked, shredded chicken (if using) and of course bacon lardons are yummy too.

Drizzle a bit more dressing over the top and serve the rest of the dressing on the side to add to the salad as you go.

MACARONI & CHEESE

SERVES 4

Break-ups, grief, job losses – for me, macaroni and cheese is the first small step in curing any emotional ailment. I like to use oat milk in my mac 'n' cheese, but only because I like the taste and texture it adds to the cheese sauce. You could make this fully vegan by using a dairy-free cheese and replacing the butter with oil (I've found coconut oil to be particularly effective). Gluten-free pasta has come on a lot as well, and I can vouch for the comfort level and deliciousness of gluten-free vegan mac 'n' cheese using this recipe.

350g (12oz) macaroni or other small pasta

30g (2 tbsp) butter

1 tbsp garlic powder

3 tbsp plain flour

500ml (2 cups) oat milk or full-fat milk

1 tsp tarragon mustard or Dijon mustard

sea salt and freshly ground black pepper

250g (2½ cups) grated mature Cheddar cheese

FOR THE BREADCRUMB TOPPING:

6–8 heaped tbsp panko or fresh breadcrumbs

a large handful of finely grated Parmesan cheese

3–4 tbsp olive oil

Preheat the oven to 180°C fan (350°F fan).

Bring a pot of salted water to a boil, then add the pasta and cook it for 2 minutes less than what the packet says so it doesn't end up overcooked. Drain and set aside.

Melt the butter in a large non-stick saucepan or casserole on a medium heat – the pan needs to be big enough to take all the pasta later. When the butter starts to foam, add the garlic powder and cook for about a minute (you could use one finely chopped garlic clove instead and cook it gently for 1 minute, but garlic powder is very handy). Add the flour to the garlic butter and stir until well combined. Cook for another minute, stirring, until you have a roux, which is a fancy name for butter and flour mixed together to make the base of a sauce.

Gradually whisk in the milk until you have a smooth sauce. Don't try to rush things here – add the milk very gradually, whisking all the time. Simmer the sauce for 5 minutes, whisking constantly, until it has thickened beautifully. Add the mustard before the sauce gets too thick so that it gets mixed in well. Season with salt and pepper.

Remove the pan from the heat, add all the Cheddar and mix until fully melted. You simply must do a taste test at this point.

Stir the cooked pasta into the cheesy sauce. Season with a generous pinch of salt and lots of cracked black pepper. Time for another taste test before transferring this molten, cheesy pasta to a large ovenproof dish or casserole.

MESSY

To make your breadcrumb topping, put the panko or fresh breadcrumbs in a large bowl with the Parmesan and olive oil and mix together. Scatter the breadcrumbs over the pasta, then bake in the preheated oven for 15–20 minutes, until the breadcrumbs are golden and the cheesy pasta is bubbling.

SOMETHING EXTRA

One of my favourite things to do with leftover mac 'n' cheese is put it in a toastie. Yes, it's as insanely indulgent as it sounds. You can either use a sandwich toaster or fry it in a pan. I also love to shallow-fry leftover mac 'n' cheese. Cut the cold, solidified mac 'n' cheese into slices, then coat it first in plain flour, then beaten egg, then breadcrumbs. Shallow-fry it in a pan with a bit of hot oil. Ridiculously good.

BLASTA BOOKS #16

BROTH IS A LOVE LANGUAGE

USING YOUR HEAD, HEART AND GUT TO SAY NO

What is your preferred love language? Are you into words of affirmation or acts of service? Do you love quality time, physical touch or gifts? I'm an All Of The Above kind of gal. Broth is also my love language. Another love language I'm trying out is saying no.

I have never felt more violently and personally attacked by a book before reading *Stop People Pleasing* by life coach Hailey Magee. 'People-pleasing,' writes Magee, 'is the act of chronically prioritising others' needs, wants, and feelings at the expense of our own needs, wants, and feelings.' She continues, 'Though the people-pleasing pattern has many origins, a common thread connects them all: the pursuit of safety.'

There's a passage in Magee's book about the over-giving and over-sharing of people-pleasers that I'm still furious about. 'Psychologists have found that kindness (which they call "healthy altruism") and people-pleasing (which they call "pathological altruism") have entirely different motives … Pathological altruists often neglect themselves in pursuit of others' well-being, and researchers have found that their actions are motivated by the desire to gain others' approval and avoid rejection.'

Those are pretty high frickin' stakes for a dinner party. No wonder we find them stressful.

Magee offers hope in the form of getting to know ourselves, then using that knowledge to create boundaries so that we can give generously without abandoning ourselves and our needs. If we can learn to help ourselves feel socially, emotionally and materially safe, argues Magee, we may be able to break that people-pleasing reflex that makes saying no so difficult.

I use food as a tool for human connection, which, as a recovering people-pleaser, means I've had to create some healthy boundaries around when and how I share food. I remind myself that I don't need to cook for everyone I meet and have a connection with. I don't need to eat things I don't want to just to prove to others that I'm a good guest or a brave eater. I don't need to neglect or disregard my own lack of energy by cooking on the beaches of Connemara for visitors.

Think about these questions as you approach cooking for a crowd. Do you want to fuss over the prep or be present at the dinner table? Is it worth overspending for a dinner party? Do you even want to cook for certain people in your life? Maybe they're more of a meet-in-a-café-for-a-coffee than a let-me-cook-you-three-courses kind of friend.

I believe true craic and pure joy require us to be connected to ourselves. Only then can we reach out and connect with others. To do this, you must protect yourself, particularly your time and energy. You must learn to listen to yourself like you listen to your loved ones when they're hurting or sad. The better we know ourselves, the more we can properly prioritise what's important to us. Sounds pretty simple, right? It's one thing to know it and another thing to do it. It takes practice and conscious effort to say no. When you are programmed to say yes, you may need some help to say no. A good method is to create a bit of space and time between the request and your answer.

The next time you are asked to do something, say, 'Thanks for asking me. Can you give me 24 hours to get back to you on this?' In that 24 hours, check in with your head, your heart and your gut. What are each of those parts of you saying about this ask? I find it helpful to write down their answers, then make an informed decision based on the information all three are telling me. Then you can decide (it might still be yes!) based on what is right for you right now, not based on an automatic response of saying a people-pleasing yes.

Another great question to ask yourself is, 'When I say yes to this (another work project, a time-consuming favour for someone, cooking an elaborate meal for practical strangers), what am I saying no to (rest time for yourself, quality time with your loved ones)?'

When we say no to the wrong things in order to say yes to the right things, we step into a better relationship with ourselves and with the world around us.

THE RECIPES

Broth is a love language.

Been dumped? Let me feed you broth. Fresh from a panic attack? Please enjoy this bowl of broth and noodles. Lost your job? Forget your sorrows in a bowl of lemony liquid.

But c'mere to me, what's the difference between a stock and a broth? Some cooks use these as interchangeable terms. Others say that broth is made with meat while stock is made with bones, and that stock is cooked for a longer amount of time. Is it wrong of me to prefer the word broth? It just hums comfort.

A great chicken stock adds deep delight to any broth or soup, and a vegetable base can be just as dreamy. I serve all my broths and liquid dinners with a spoonful of White Mausu peanut rayu, and their smoky chilli oil is my new favourite thing (both are available online). I also love the iconic OG chilli oil, Lao Gan Ma Crispy Chilli Oil, which you can get in any Asian food store.

ALL-ROUNDER ROAST CHICKEN

SERVES 2–4

The first step in making a great chicken broth is a great roast chicken, so here's a foolproof recipe for a roast chicken that can be made on a Sunday and brought forward into meals throughout the week, including your broths.

1 whole free-range and/or organic chicken

1 whole garlic bulb, cut in half around the middle

1 lemon, cut in half around the middle

1–2 olive oil

sea salt and freshly cracked black pepper

Preheat your oven to 180°C fan (350°F fan).

Put your whole chicken in a wide, shallow casserole or a roasting tin. Add the halved garlic and any loose little unpeeled cloves around the chicken.

Squeeze the juice from the lemon over the chicken, then toss the squeezed-out halves into the roasting tin.

Drizzle some olive oil over the chicken, then sprinkle 2–3 tablespoons of sea salt over the chicken (this helps its skin go crispy) and crack some black pepper over the top.

Roast in the preheated oven for 1 hour 20 minutes, until the internal temperature of the thigh hits 75°C (165°F). If you don't have a digital thermometer, pierce the thigh with a sharp knife or skewer. If the juices run clear, it's done.

Take the chicken out of the oven and let it rest for at least 20 minutes. This is an important step – it lets the chicken chill out and reabsorb all its own cooking juices – so don't be tempted to skip it!

Carve your chicken and serve with roast vegetables, as part of a salad (like the Caesar salad on page 23) or in a broth.

Once the rest of the chicken is nice and cool, remove all the meat from the bones. Instead of throwing away the bones, use them to make the beautiful chicken stock on the next page to add to your soups.

HOMEMADE CHICKEN STOCK

MAKES APPROX. 1 LITRE (4¼ CUPS)

the leftover carcass from 1 whole roast chicken (page 28)

1 onion, unpeeled and cut in half

1 carrot, roughly chopped

1 leek or celery stick, roughly chopped

1 whole garlic bulb, cut in half around the middle

a handful of fresh herbs like parsley and/or thyme

1 lemon, cut in half around the middle

1 tsp sea salt

1 tsp black peppercorns

Put all the ingredients in a large saucepan and pour in 2 litres (8½ cups) of water.

Bring to a boil, then turn down the heat and simmer for 1–3 hours. If cooking it for more than 1 hour, keep the pan partially covered with a lid to stop the liquid from reducing too much. The longer you let it simmer, the better the flavour, in my experience. But once I left mine on for such a long simmer, uncovered, that when I came back all the liquid had disappeared! It was a sad day.

Once you're happy with the flavour of the broth, take the pan off the heat. Strain it through a sieve into a storage container or use it straight away in a soup or as a broth base.

This should keep in your fridge for up to a week and for up to three months in the freezer.

VEGETABLE STOCK

To make a homemade vegetable stock, just leave out the chicken carcass and double the quantity of veggies. Or even better, take Conor Spacey's advice in *Blasta Books #7: Wasted* to freeze all your odds and ends of raw veg until you have enough to fill a big freezerproof bag, then cook as above with the garlic, herbs, lemon, salt and pepper.

LEMON & ORZO SOUP

SERVES 2

This is an adaptation from one of my all-time favourite cookbooks, *The First Mess*, by Canadian food writer and blogger Laura Wright. I've learned so much about adding flavour and depth with vegan-friendly ingredients, particularly the magic of miso. The original recipe uses white miso, but I make this with whatever miso I have to hand. I've tweaked Laura's original recipe slightly and have added chicken and greens.

2 tbsp olive oil

1 onion, thinly sliced (I use a red onion for colour)

3 garlic cloves, crushed

a thumb-sized piece of fresh ginger, peeled and finely chopped or grated

1 tbsp ground turmeric

800ml (3⅓ cups) chicken or vegetable stock (page 29 or from stock cubes)

200g (1 cup) orzo

½ lemon, sliced into 3–4 rounds

1 heaped tbsp miso

1 tsp apple cider vinegar

sea salt and freshly ground black pepper

a large handful of kale leaves, finely shredded

leftover roast chicken (page 28; optional)

Heat the olive oil in a large saucepan on a medium-high heat. Add the onion and cook for about 5 minutes, until starting to soften. Add the garlic, ginger, turmeric and a splash of stock so the ginger doesn't stick to the bottom of the pan. Cook for 1–2 minutes, until lovely and fragrant. Add the orzo, stirring to coat it in the spices, then add the lemon slices and pour in the rest of the stock.

Mix the miso and apple cider vinegar together in a small bowl, then add a bit of the stock to help the miso dissolve fully. Add this to the saucepan, then season with salt and pepper. Cover the pot and simmer, still on a medium-high heat, for 7–9 minutes, until the orzo is fully cooked.

When you're ready to serve, divide the finely shredded kale and leftover chicken (if using) between your serving bowls, then pour over spoonfuls of the hot orzo broth. Or you can add the kale and chicken (if using) directly to the broth at this stage to warm them up. I do it the former way so the chicken and greens don't get overcooked, and because I don't mind food not being piping hot – I actually prefer it if it's not because I can taste more.

Just FYI, if you leave the orzo alone in the soup for too long, the orzo will soak up all the broth. It loves it! If this happens, or if you're eating leftovers, just add a good splash of water to loosen it back up.

TO GARNISH:

a small handful of fresh herbs, such as mint, parsley, dill, thyme or whatever you have, chopped

1–2 spring onions, thinly sliced (optional)

peanut rayu or chilli oil

To serve, divide between two bowls and garnish with some chopped fresh herbs and thinly sliced spring onion if you have it. Top with your favourite chilli oil – mine is the Irish-made White Mausu peanut rayu, but I also love the OG Lao Gan Ma chilli oil.

MISO & MUSHROOM BROTH

SERVES 2

Anstice and I make this about once a week for each other all throughout the year. It makes us feel loved and cared for. My current obsession is doenjang, a Korean soybean paste that has a saltier, funkier flavour than miso. Just swap the miso for doenjang and see which one you prefer. You can make it fully vegetarian, which we often do, but if you've roasted a chicken and made a broth with the bones, they are welcome in this recipe too.

2 tbsp olive oil

100g (3½oz) button or chestnut mushrooms, thinly sliced

2 garlic cloves, finely chopped or grated

a thumb-sized piece of fresh ginger, peeled and finely chopped or grated

800ml (3⅓ cups) chicken or vegetable stock (page 29 or from stock cubes)

1 tbsp miso or doenjang

1 lemon, cut in half

about 100g (4oz) ramen noodles

100g (3½oz) firm tofu, cut into cubes

a large handful of greens, like pak choi or kale, finely shredded

leftover roast chicken (page 28; optional)

TO GARNISH:
1 spring onion, thinly sliced

1 tsp black sesame seeds

peanut rayu or chilli oil

Heat the oil in a large saucepan on a medium heat. Add the sliced mushrooms and cook gently for about 10 minutes, until soft. Add a little more oil if you need to, but keep in mind that the mushrooms will absorb oil before releasing it again once they're cooked. Add the garlic and ginger and cook for another minute or two, until they've softened a bit – be careful not to burn them. Pour in the stock.

Mix the miso or doenjang with 1 tablespoon of the hot broth and the juice of half of the lemon, then stir this into the pan. Simmer for about 20 minutes, until the flavours have started to get to know each other.

When you're ready to serve, cook your noodles according to the packet instructions, then drain. You can use less or more noodles depending on how carby you're feeling.

Divide the cooked ramen noodles, tofu, finely shredded greens and leftover chicken (if using) between your two serving bowls, then pour the hot broth over the top. Garnish with the spring onion and black sesame seeds and finish with a drizzle of rayu or chilli oil. Slice the leftover lemon into wedges and serve on the side.

SPICY COCONUT NOODLE SOUP

SERVES 2

My friend Zoe made me a version of this soup about 15 years ago. It was so delicious that I've been trying to recreate it ever since.

1 small sweet potato, unpeeled and cut into wedges

2 tbsp vegetable oil, plus extra for roasting

sea salt and freshly ground black pepper

1 small white onion, thinly sliced

4 garlic cloves, peeled and left whole

a thumb-sized piece of fresh ginger, peeled and finely diced

1 tsp dried chilli flakes

2 tbsp ground turmeric

1 tsp ground cumin

1 tsp ground coriander

1 x 400ml (14fl oz) tin of coconut milk

about 400ml (1 2/3 cups) chicken or vegetable stock (page 29)

1 lime, cut in half

about 100g (4oz) vermicelli rice noodles or ramen noodles

a large handful of kale leaves, stalks removed and finely shredded

leftover roast chicken (page 28; optional)

TO GARNISH:

fresh coriander leaves

1 spring onion, thinly sliced

smoky chilli oil

Preheat your oven to 180°C fan (350°F fan).

Put the sweet potato wedges on a baking tray, drizzle with a little oil and season well, tossing to coat. Roast in the preheated oven for 30–40 minutes, until cooked through. Set aside.

Meanwhile, heat the 2 tablespoons of oil in a large saucepan on a medium heat. Add the onion and garlic and cook for about 10 minutes, until soft. Lower the heat, add the ginger and chilli flakes and cook gently for 1–2 minutes, just until the ginger is fragrant, being careful not to burn it.

Add the turmeric, cumin, coriander and a splash of coconut milk and mix well. Cook for 1 minute before adding the rest of the coconut milk and the stock. Squeeze in the juice of half of the lime. Let the soup bubble away, uncovered, for 15–20 minutes, until it has reduced a little bit.

When you're ready to serve, cook your noodles according to the packet instructions, then drain

Divide the roasted sweet potato, cooked noodles, finely shredded kale and leftover chicken (if using) between your two serving bowls, then pour the hot broth over the top to heat the chicken and wilt the kale. Garnish with fresh coriander leaves and thinly sliced spring onion and finish with a drizzle of smoky chilli oil. Slice the other half of the lime into wedges and serve on the side.

BLASTA BOOKS #16

CRAIC IN THE KITCHEN
(AKA PARTY FOOD)

PRIORITY PIZZA PIE

There's a well-known coaching tool called The Wheel of Life attributed to life coach Paul J. Meyer that I use all the time with coaching clients and on a weekly basis to figure out my own life. I like to call it a priority pizza pie because pizza is life.

1 Draw a big circle on a sheet of paper – a pizza base, if you will – and divide the circle into eight slices.

2 In each slice, write a key category, area or purpose in your life right now. It could be family, mental health, physical health, work, hobbies – whatever is most important to you. You can include things you want to prioritise but aren't managing to get to right now. And it's okay if you don't have eight slices – your pizza might currently have four or six.

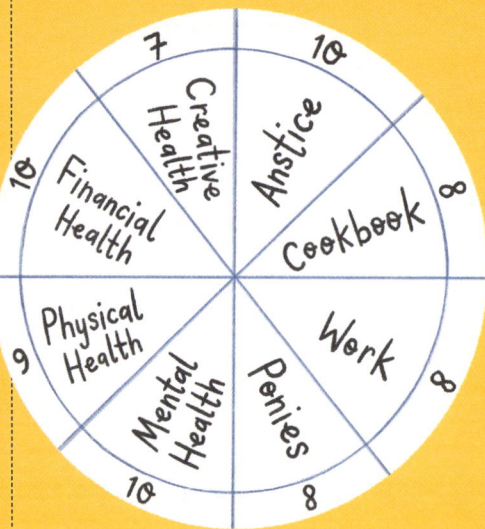

3 On the crust of each slice, write a number between 1 and 10 to reflect how important this area is to you, with 1 being not important at all and 10 being extremely important. You aren't ranking these – they could all be 10s, while some might be a 7 or others might be a 4 or a 9.

4 Now think about how much time and energy you're currently putting into each area. Write a number on the slice – 1 for basically no time and energy and 10 for all the time and energy available to you. Colour each slice to reflect that number – for example, if it's a 5, colour it in halfway; if it's a 10, colour the whole slice.

5 Take a step back from your priority pizza pie. What is it telling you about the balance of your life right now? What areas are taking up most of your time and energy? Do you need to shift your energy and focus to give more to other areas? If all the toppings are on just one or two slices, well, that's not very appetising. Just like a good pizza, the time and energy you put into the important areas of your life are most effective when they're well balanced too.

At the beginning of the month, I do my top eight priorities, then on a weekly basis I make sure they're being tended to. Every week, I make it a bit smaller and divide it into four slices. At the beginning of the week, I remind myself what my top four priorities are, then I make sure they're on the list and getting attention.

THE RECIPES

When my battery pack is full and my priority pizza pie is nicely balanced, I love to cook for a crowd. It's a challenge, an expression of creativity, a juggling of timings and parts and elements. When I get it all right, it's enormously rewarding. At the wrong moment in time, however, when energy is low and anxiety is high, trying to cook for a gang of pals is overstimulating, stressful and exhausting.

So how do you ensure craic in the kitchen? Like all good cooking, a key ingredient is timing. Not just the timing of the cooking, but the timing of your life. When is the best time of the month for you to invite friends over? What time of day works best for you? Do you prefer a brunch, an evening gathering or maybe even all-day affairs?

The best way to host is to meet people where they are, and to invite them to do the same with you. If they arrive and you've burned the cake that was meant to be dessert, let them in on the joke. The people who mind don't matter, and the people who matter don't mind.

The recipes in this section make up one of my favourite menus for having people over, designed to keep sweating and stress to a minimum. There's lots you can make ahead, so you're not chained to the cooker while your guests arrive. Plus there are lots of crossover ingredients, so your shopping list isn't huge – almonds turn up in the stew and in the dessert, as do mint and pomegranate, while tahini is in the starter and main course. And I give you full permission to buy key ingredients, such as the beetroot hummus or the meringues, rather than make everything from scratch. Match your cooking to your capacity, not to your expectations.

TOP TIPS FOR COOKING FOR A CROWD

1. Don't bite off more than you can chew. Serve something you've made before – that way, you'll know how long it takes and how yummy it will be.

2. Do the shopping the day before to save your energy for cooking but also for hosting. The whole point of having your pals over for dinner is to have the craic and connect with them, which is hard to do if you're exhausted after fighting against perfectionism and unrealistic expectations.

3. Make things ahead if you can.

4. There is no shame in not making things from scratch! This includes dips, crackers, dessert, whatever – let the professionals help you.

5. It's completely fine to change your mind at the last minute and order in or get a couple of pizzas out of the freezer.

6. Clean as you go. This is something I have yet to master, but thankfully Anstice cleans as I go and that works for us.

7. Delegation is delicious. Give people jobs. Accept help if it's offered. Make chopping a communal experience, not a painful martyrdom that's no fun for anyone.

8. Once that last morsel of food has been enjoyed, your job is done. Let your friends or partner or children or roommate do the washing-up or leave it till later (ideally tomorrow).

9. Don't forget to eat! It's easy to get so carried away with the prep and the hosting and the tablescaping and the seating plan that you might overlook enjoying the food you have prepared and, even more importantly, enjoying the time with your guests.

10. Never apologise to your guests about how bad your food is or how it tasted better the last time you made it. And remember, there is no such thing as perfect. You're not on *MasterChef*. There is no dramatic narrator doing a voiceover to your cooking. (Although if a dramatic commentary is something you find motivating, perhaps one of your guests or loved ones could oblige.)

STARTER
SMOKED MACKEREL BITES WITH BEETROOT DIP

SERVES 6 (WITH LEFTOVER DIP)

It's tempting to call this beetroot hummus, but did you know that the word *hummus* translates from Arabic to English as *chickpea*? I suppose you could put chickpeas in this and call it beetroot hummus, but this version is technically a dip, for those of you taking notes in the back.

I sometimes make this with fresh beetroot by roasting them beforehand. The flavour is sweeter, but vacuum-packed beets are perfectly yummy. I also encourage you to buy beetroot hummus for your dinner party. Go a step further and buy a gorgeous pre-made smoked mackerel pâté. There's no shame in shortcuts, especially when you're cooking for a crowd.

2 good-quality smoked mackerel fillets

½ loaf of brown soda bread, caraway brown bread (page 18) or seedy loaf (page 19), cut into bite-sized pieces

shop-bought horseradish sauce

a handful of fresh chives, very finely chopped

1 lemon, cut into small wedges

FOR THE BEETROOT DIP:

2 big handfuls of walnuts

500g (18oz) vacuum-packed beetroot, cut into halves or quarters

juice of 2 lemons

2 tbsp tahini

2 tbsp garlic powder

sea salt and freshly cracked black pepper

To make the beetroot dip, start by toasting the walnuts in a dry frying pan on a medium heat. This will take around 5 minutes, but keep an eye on them because they can burn suddenly.

Put the toasted walnuts in your food processor along with the beetroot, lemon juice, tahini, garlic powder and a generous pinch of salt and freshly cracked black pepper. Blitz until smooth. You can add a little water if needed, a few drops at a time, to help blend the beetroot. You can make this a day or two in advance and there will be plenty of beetroot dip left over for you to enjoy after the party.

When you're ready to assemble, pull the skin off the smoked mackerel fillets. Try to use the best-quality smoked mackerel you can get – here in Ireland, I love Connemara Smokehouse's wild peppered smoked mackerel. Use a fork to shred the mackerel, being extra careful to remove any little pin bones.

Add a dollop of beetroot dip to each little piece of bread, then top with some shredded smoked mackerel. Add a teaspoon of horseradish sauce on top, then a sprinkling of finely chopped chives. Finish with a squeeze of lemon juice and an extra little pinch of salt and pepper just before serving on a big platter so everyone can help themselves.

MESSY

TRY THIS

It's always a good idea to have something on the table for your guests to nibble on when they arrive, so I put some beetroot dip in a bowl, sprinkled with chopped fresh mint, to serve with crudités. Add a sprinkle of salt and a squeeze of lemon juice to your carrots, a tasty trick my brother Peter picked up in his travels around the Balkans.

MAIN COURSE
SLOW-COOKED BEEF & HARISSA STEW
SERVES 6

This dish has been with me for many years. It's an adaptation of a Sarah Buenfeld recipe on the BBC Good Food website, a resource that was one of my main cooking teachers. What I love about this recipe is its use of harissa – you can tone it down or dial it up, spice-wise – and how the heat is balanced by the ground almonds.

It's lovely at Christmastime, especially with a bit of added cinnamon (just throw a couple of whole sticks into the stew), but it's fantastic at any time of year. It's easily doubled if you have a pot that's big enough, and it gets better the longer you cook it. Just make sure you top it up with stock if you're going for a long, slow cook.

2 tbsp sunflower oil

1kg (2¼lb) good-quality stewing beef (the better the quality, the better the taste and texture) – I recommend using beef chuck and neck pieces

1 onion, diced

6–8 garlic cloves, peeled, left whole and crushed

a thumb-sized piece of ginger, peeled and diced

1–2 tbsp harissa, depending on how spicy you want your stew to be

1 tsp ground cumin or cumin seeds

1.5 litres (2½ pints) beef stock

2 heaped tbsp ground almonds

sea salt and freshly cracked black pepper

Heat the sunflower oil in a large heavy-based pot or casserole on a medium-high heat. Working in batches so that you don't overcrowd the pot (two batches will usually do it), add the beef and cook until it's browned and starting to caramelise. This caramelisation is the first step in a deeply flavourful stew. Use a slotted spoon to transfer to a bowl while you cook the rest.

Reduce the heat to medium. There should be some beef juices left in the pan, which you can cook the onion and garlic in for 10 minutes, until the onions are softened and translucent. Add the ginger and cook for another 2 minutes. Add the harissa and cumin and cook for 1–2 minutes.

Add the beef back to the pot, mixing everything together well. Pour in the beef stock, add the ground almonds and give everything another good mix. Season generously with salt and freshly cracked black pepper.

Bring the stew to a boil, then reduce the heat to a steady simmer. Cook, uncovered, for 3 hours, until the meat is very, very tender. Add more beef stock if the stew is looking dry. You can also cover the pot and let it cook for even longer if you have time. The stew can be made the day before – just add a little more stock to reheat to keep the stew from drying out.

TO GARNISH:

tahini sauce (page 44)

3 tbsp pomegranate seeds

2 tbsp toasted flaked almonds

a handful of fresh mint leaves, chopped

When the stew is ready, drizzle some tahini sauce on top, then scatter over the pomegranate seeds and toasted flaked almonds. Finish with a generous sprinkling of chopped fresh mint and serve straight to the table.

MAIN COURSE
QUEEN CAULIFLOWER
SERVES 4 AS A MAIN OR 6 AS A SIDE

I call this Queen Cauliflower because it's an appropriately regal main course for vegetarians or vegans, and it also works as a delicious side for the beef and harissa stew on page 40. I co-created this recipe with my friends Robbie and Jessie, who share my adoration of cauliflower, especially when paired with tahini. Robbie even goes the extra mile and keeps the cauliflower whole for a showstopper presentation. If you want to give that a go, steam the whole cauliflower for 10–15 minutes, then roast it for 30–45 minutes.

1 head of cauliflower

olive oil

1 lemon

sea salt and freshly cracked black pepper

TO GARNISH:

tahini sauce (page 44)

3 tbsp pomegranate seeds

2 tbsp toasted flaked almonds

a handful of fresh mint leaves, chopped

Preheat your oven to 160°C fan (325°F fan).

If creating a main course fit for a queen, cut the cauliflower into quarters, keeping the leaves on – they go deliciously crispy when roasted in the oven. Cut into six wedges if you're serving this as a side.

Put the cauliflower in a roasting tin. Drizzle olive oil all over the cauliflower, then squeeze over the juice of the lemon. Season generously with salt and freshly cracked black pepper, especially the salt, because that will help the cauliflower go crispy.

Roast in the preheated oven for 45–60 minutes, until al dente and crispy but not burned. If you prefer a softer cauliflower, you can cover it with foil for the first 45 minutes, then remove it and roast it uncovered for a further 30 minutes.

When the cauliflower is ready to serve, transfer the wedges to a serving platter and drizzle tahini sauce generously on top. Scatter over the pomegranate seeds and toasted flaked almonds, then finish with a generous sprinkling of chopped fresh mint.

SIDES
BUTTERED GREENS

SERVES 6

While arguably not everyone's cup of tea, I love nothing more than a big bowl of dark greens on my dinner table. They go with basically everything and balance heavier dishes like mac 'n' cheese or a slow-cooked beef stew.

3 large handfuls of greens – kale, spinach, chard, all your favourites

a generous knob of butter

1 lemon wedge

sea salt and freshly cracked black pepper

Thinly slice the greens into shreds, stalks and all.

Melt a generous knob of butter in a large non-stick frying pan on a medium-high heat. When the butter starts to foam, add the shredded greens and cook, stirring occasionally, for 5–8 minutes, until the greens are wilted and cooked through but still bright green and al dente.

Serve immediately with a squeeze of lemon and a big pinch of salt and pepper.

SIDES
TAHINI SAUCE

MAKES APPROX. 120ML (½ CUP)

Using soft, sweet roasted garlic makes this sauce to die for. You can use garlic powder, grated raw garlic or even a shop-bought garlic paste instead, but the roasted garlic makes it extra-special.

1 whole head of garlic

olive oil, for drizzling

juice of 1 lemon

6 heaped tbsp natural yogurt

1–2 heaped tbsp tahini

sea salt and freshly cracked black pepper

2–3 tbsp water

Preheat the oven to 160°C fan (325°F fan).

Cut the garlic bulb in half around the middle, leaving the skin on. Put the two halves on a baking tray, cut sides up. Drizzle a bit of oil over the top and roast in the preheated oven for 45–60 minutes, until soft and roasted but not burned – burned garlic is bitter garlic. Remove it from the oven and allow to cool. Use a fork or your fingers to squeeze the soft cloves out of their skins, then crush them to a paste.

Put the garlic paste in a bowl with the lemon juice, yogurt and tahini and season with salt and pepper. Whisk together, then add 1 tablespoon of water and whisk again. You want the sauce to have a drizzling consistency, so add 1–2 more tablespoons of water if needed.

Serve drizzled on top of the beef stew on page 40 and the roasted cauliflower on page 42. I love this sauce and also use it as a salad dressing for shredded raw Brussels sprouts with toasted almonds and pomegranate seeds. If I'm roasting a chicken, it's a gorgeous alternative to gravy when paired with a Middle Eastern side like couscous. Roast some aubergines and serve them with this sauce drizzled on top. The possibilities are endless.

TOP TIP
If you're using this sauce for the Queen Cauliflower on page 42, you can roast the garlic alongside the cauliflower.

SIDES
SMUSHED SPUDS
SERVES 6

Roast spuds need a hot oven, so these can be made a few hours in advance, then reheated just before serving so that you can roast the cauliflower on page 42 at a lower heat. If you happen to have two ovens, you can cook the spuds and cauliflower simultaneously, but the spuds are yummy even if they're allowed to sit for an hour or two.

1.5kg (3lb 5oz) baby potatoes

olive oil

sea salt and freshly cracked black pepper

TO GARNISH
a handful of fresh chives, finely chopped

Put the whole baby spuds in a big pot and cover them with cold water. Bring to a boil and cook for 10–12 minutes, until the potatoes are cooked through but not falling apart. Drain and allow to cool.

Preheat your oven to 200°C fan (400°F fan).

Transfer the spuds to a large roasting tin (or two tins if needed). Use the bottom of a regular drinking glass to smush each potato so it breaks apart a bit, but not too much. Some potatoes won't break at all, but that's okay. They're tough lil' guys and can stay whole.

Drizzle your spuds generously with oil and season with lots of salt and pepper. Roast in the hot oven for at least 20 minutes, but ideally closer to 40 minutes, or to your preferred levels of crispiness.

Set aside until ready to serve. You can reheat them in the oven (not the microwave, they'll lose their crisp!) for 5 minutes.

Transfer to a serving platter, sprinkle some finely chopped chives on top and season with a bit more salt and pepper.

DESSERT
NONCHALANT MERINGUES
SERVES 6

When cooking for a crowd, I usually buy dessert rather than make it. The truth is, I'm not a great baker. This isn't false modesty. I am easily distracted under pressure and regularly forget ingredients or get the measurements spectacularly wrong. Since baking is typically less forgiving than cooking, it's often better for my guests if I let the professionals handle the end of the meal.

You could of course make your own meringues instead of buying them, like I do. More power to you! They're a great make-ahead option. It's completely up to you and your energy levels. Would you enjoy making the extra effort or is that going to tip you over the edge into a meringue-fuelled meltdown? You're the boss of your meringue destiny.

350g (12oz) strawberries (or raspberries or whatever fruit is in season)

1 tbsp caster sugar

1 lemon wedge

180ml (¾ cup) double cream

6–8 shop-bought mini meringue nests

a handful of toasted flaked almonds

a handful of fresh mint, finely chopped

Start by removing the stems from the strawberries, then slicing the strawberries into a large bowl. Add the sugar and a squeeze of lemon juice and gently toss to coat. Allow to sit on the countertop for at least 1 hour before using. This will transform the strawberries into their best, softest, sweetest versions of themselves, plus it will create a little strawberry juice for drizzling.

Whip your double cream until it's the consistency you like. I prefer a loose, softly whipped cream that's just about setting, but others like a firmer cream.

When you're ready to serve, arrange the meringues on a serving plate. Add a dollop of whipped cream on top of each one, then divide the strawberries evenly among the meringues, drizzling the strawberry juice on top too.

Finish with a sprinkling of toasted flaked almonds and chopped fresh mint. Serve immediately.

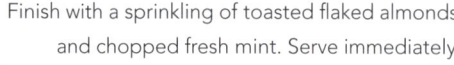

CHEESE COURSE
BISCUITS FOR CHEESE
MAKES APPROX. 22

Anstice's mum, Caroline, is a wonderful cook and I enjoy being her sous-chef. Visits to her home are always marked by exquisite meals from start to finish, such as these delightful biscuits to serve with cheese.

Caroline's top tip for this recipe is the addition of olive oil, which gives the biscuits a slightly softer texture and is a little easier on one's teeth.

a knob of butter, for greasing

150g (1 cup) whole almonds, roughly chopped

120g (1 cup) plain flour, plus extra for dusting

100g (¾ cup) dried cranberries

50g (¼ cup) dark brown sugar

4–5 dried figs, finely chopped

½ tsp sea salt

¼ tsp baking soda

240ml (1 cup) milk

2 tbsp olive oil

Preheat the oven to 160°C fan (325°F fan). Butter and flour the bottoms and sides of a 450g (1lb) loaf tin.

Put the almonds, flour, cranberries, brown sugar, figs, salt and baking soda in a large bowl and stir to combine. Mix the milk and olive oil together, then pour them into the dry ingredients and stir to create a batter. Pour the batter into the prepared loaf tin.

Bake in the preheated oven for 50 minutes, until golden brown. Remove from the oven and cool completely in the loaf tin on a wire cooling rack. If you start to cut the loaf before it has completely cooled, it will crumble and you won't be able to cut it as thinly as you need to.

Once the loaf has completely cooled, preheat the oven again to 180°C fan (350°F fan). Line a baking sheet with non-stick baking paper.

Remove the loaf from the pan. Use a sharp serrated knife to cut the loaf into approximately 22 thin slices – as thin as you dare. Arrange the slices in a single layer on the baking sheet. Bake in the oven for 15–20 minutes, flipping them over halfway through, until golden brown on both sides. Transfer to the cooling rack to cool completely before serving alongside a cheeseboard (page 48).

Store at room temperature in an airtight container for up to one week if they haven't all been eaten by then.

CHEESE COURSE

AN EASY CHEESEBOARD

Anstice and I dream of someday owning a few naughty goats or a couple of docile bovines to milk for making cheese, and we've been gradually accruing knowledge on the topic. We worked at a goat farm in Portugal for a month, we do some occasional milking for a farmer with a couple of goats in Connemara, and I had the privilege of doing a course at Ballymaloe Cookery School with David Asher, an expert in natural cheesemaking.

To better understand cheesemaking, we also volunteered at Gubbeen Farmhouse for a few days and got elbow deep in the cheese vats. We've visited Cáis na Tíre in County Tipperary and we've met the beautiful goats at St Tola in County Clare. Most of our research into cheese, however, has been through eating it.

Serving a cheeseboard at the end of a meal is an easy way to bring a dinner party to a close. The French like to serve their cheese before dessert, which is deeply sensible, but I've become accustomed to how we do it in Ireland and elsewhere and serve cheese after dessert. As a cook, a final cheese course tells me the meal is over and my work is done, particularly because I never do the washing up. That is not my job.

I believe in the magic power of three, so when assembling a cheeseboard I generally go for a hard cheese (like a Comté or Cheddar), a soft cheese (like a Camembert or Brie) and a blue cheese. It's fun to have a mix of cow's milk, sheep's milk and goat's milk cheeses too.

Personally (and somewhat controversially), I think many chutneys, while delicious, can overpower cheese, so I prefer to have some local raw honey on my cheeseboard instead. I love the classic bunch of grapes draped over a hunk of cheese, but another gorgeous addition is sliced fresh apples or pears, dried figs or dates, all huddled together and interspersed with crackers and biscuits for cheese. Serve with a selection of cheese knives and make sure everyone's glasses of wine, beer or non-alcoholic alternative are topped up.

MESSY

MESSY ESSAY

LIVING YOUR BEST LIFE IN THE GREAT OUTDOORS

YOUR BEST IS GOOD ENOUGH, EVEN WHEN IT'S NOT GREAT

It's remarkable how delicious a simple sausage sandwich on white bread with brown sauce can taste when you're eating it on a beach. Almost anything you eat outdoors, especially when seasoned with a fresh sea swim or a long hike, tastes amazing. The environment is so conducive to eating, and can be so much fun to cook in.

My favourite place to cook is beside the sea, especially on the Connemara coastline of the West of Ireland where I live. Like any self-respecting cook, I enjoy cooking over an open fire. After all, cooking over fire is what made us human, according to anthropologist and primatologist Richard Wrangham. Sure, you can go full Francis Mallmann and build a Patagonian fire pit if you have the private property or permission to do so, but let's pare things back and keep it simple, shall we?

When cooking outdoors, I usually keep the fire contained to a little gas camping stove. When the opportunity for a beachside buffet presents itself, I grab my picnic bag, my Le Creuset pot and some fresh ingredients and head to the shoreline.

I love feeling the sun on my shoulders as I crouch over a pot of something simple sizzling by the seaside. I love finding just the right coastal rock with a flat, level surface to set up a makeshift kitchen on, and a wind shelter for the flame. I like having all my little bits and pieces of spices and fresh herbs and putting my Opinel vegetable knife to good use.

As a little kid, did you ever camp outside in your back garden in a shonky tent or sleep overnight in the living room underneath a sheet fort, imagining that you were under a blanket of stars in a wild desert? The absolute craic of it. As adults, we tend not to give ourselves permission to create and access that kind of simple, silly make-believe.

The joy of cooking outdoors is that it's anti-perfectionism. It typically requires adaptability and creativity because there are clear limitations. You may be working with one little gas stove, so you may be limited to one-pot wonders; you may have to improvise if you forget a key ingredient; sand may fly into the stew, but you must carry on. When in Connemara, it may start raining sideways halfway through the cooking process. Even within those limitations, the possibilities for adventure are endless. It's fun, freeing, imperfect, sweet, innocent and unfussy.

For me, cooking outdoors taps into that feeling of possibility and adventure, and part of its success is because it invites you to go back to basics. It gives you the freedom of limiting choice, because you can't access your usual supplies or tools at an outdoor cookout and you can't pack your whole kitchen with you (although you may, like me, bring your Le Creuset).

My go-to dish for cooking outdoors is my campfire stew (page 56), a tomato-based stew with beans, eggs and fresh herbs on top. I might extend my beachside menu to a bit of fresh fish blackened in a frying pan or freshly shucked oysters, but I tend to keep it simple because a little goes a long way. Going back to that sausage sandwich, limiting your choices can actually feel freeing.

In *Paradox of Choice: Why More Is Less* (2004), American psychologist Barry Schwartz writes that 'the existence of multiple alternatives makes it easy for us to imagine alternatives that don't exist – alternatives that combine the attractive features of the ones that do exist. And to the extent that we engage our imaginations in this way, we will be even less satisfied with the alternative we end up choosing. So, once again, a greater variety of choices actually makes us feel worse.'

We're constantly bombarded with messages of more is more. It is the capitalist way, and it takes a lot of conscious effort to reject those messages. The wellness industry, aka Diet Culture 2.0, depends on selling you an idea of your Best Self and your Best Life. That if you can just get to The Perfect Version of yourself, then, and only then, will you be happy. Toxic positivity and pernicious aspiration, however well-intentioned, are soaked in privilege and ableism, creating unrealistic and unattainable notions of what we should be getting out of our lives. It's exhausting.

Maybe you'll hate outdoor cooking. Maybe having the crunch of sand in your sausage sandwich is a deal breaker for you. Maybe the idea of bringing more than just a towel to the beach seems like too much. That's okay. You do you.

I have my own version of my Best Life, and it changes daily. I try to embrace my capacity. In the space of a month, a week or even a day sometimes, I can feel tremendous highs and debilitating slumps. So I ask myself, 'What does my Best Life look like *today*?' As a recovering perfectionist, I'm learning that my best is good enough, even when it's not great. Feck great. I'm aiming for slightly above average.

BLASTA BOOKS #16

THE RECIPES

When cooking beachside, I regularly make my campfire stew (page 56), but my one-pot pasta (page 12), lemon and orzo soup (page 30), miso and mushroom broth (page 32) and spicy coconut noodle soup (page 33) can all be easily made outdoors too. Basically, anything that doesn't require a rigidly specific temperature works well (little gas stoves are brilliant, but it can be hard to regulate their temperature).

I regularly take my Le Creuset casserole to the seaside. It's outrageously heavy and my picnic pals laugh at me for doing it ... until they taste what comes out of it. Then they, too, realise it was worth schlepping it down to the beach.

MUST-HAVES FOR COOKING OUTDOORS

Anstice and I have a box that we keep stocked and ready to go for when the grá for a beach cookout hits us. Anstice cleverly put our favourite spices (garlic powder, smoked paprika, cumin, chilli flakes) in 50ml (2fl oz) travel pots, which makes them easy to transport. We also keep a chopping board, Opinel vegetable knife, Microplane grater, tea towel, bin bags, picnic blanket, cutlery, wooden spoon, olive oil, brown sugar, and salt and pepper in the box. Then all we need is some fresh water for cooking and cleaning and our portable gas stove (plus an extra gas canister in case we run out) and we're good to go.

A picnic table and chairs are handy for cooking and eating on, but they're not a must. Making a makeshift kitchen space out of ancient coastal rock formations is even more fun.

It goes without saying that you must follow local rules and guidelines around having an open fire or a gas stove when cooking outdoors.

BLASTA BOOKS #16

PEANUT BUTTER & CHOCOLATE-DIPPED DATES

MAKES 12

A sea-swimming pal, Noreen, made a version of these for our swimming group many moons ago. I love taking these with me to the seaside for a treat after an icy dip. They're also great for cooler-weather hikes (they tend to melt in the heat) and they're also delightful to have as a treat in a camper-van.

about 50g (1¾oz) chocolate (I like dark, but use your favourite)

12 dates, pitted

12 tsp peanut butter or your favourite nut butter

flaky sea salt

Break the chocolate into small pieces and put them in a heatproof bowl. Melt the chocolate in a microwave, stirring every 30 seconds or so, or you can sit the bowl on top of a pot of gently simmering water, making sure the water doesn't touch the bottom of the bowl. Keep the pot on a low heat and stir the chocolate with a spatula or wooden spoon until it has completely melted.

Meanwhile, fill each date with a teaspoon of peanut butter.

Get a baking tray or large chopping board ready for the dates by putting a piece of non-stick baking paper on top of it.

Dip each date into the melted chocolate, then put it on the lined tray or chopping board and do the rest. You can completely cover the dates in chocolate, cover half of them or cover just the bottom so that you can see the peanut butter.

Sprinkle each chocolate-covered date with a tiny pinch of sea salt. Chill the dates in the fridge for at least an hour or overnight, until the chocolate is completely cooled and set.

Pack them in an airtight container with a bit of baking paper between the layers so they don't stick together. Keep them in a cool, dry place until you're ready to eat.

MALTY MUESLI BARS

MAKES 12

A sturdy dessert is a must in an outdoor setting or camper-van adventure. A delicate pavlova, as those who have tried will know, doesn't travel as well as a hefty flapjack. You need a sweet treat that can be stuffed into a backpack, and one that will keep for the length of your trip in a biscuit tin or airtight container.

Anstice's Aunt Joanie and Uncle Johnny shared this recipe with us when we visited them in New Zealand. These malty muesli bars are the ultimate hike treat – they kept us going on a four-day trek of the Abel Tasman Coast Track, despite some of our stash being stolen by an opportunistic weka bird.

200g (7oz) salted butter

1 tbsp malt extract (molasses or honey are both good substitutes)

6 Weetabix, crushed

100g (½ cup) light brown sugar

80g (1 cup) rolled oats

80g (½ cup) pumpkin seeds

70g (⅓ cup) sunflower seeds

60g (½ cup) self-raising flour

60g (½ cup) dried cranberries

50g (½ cup) Ovaltine

1 tsp baking powder

Preheat your oven to 180°C fan (350°F fan). Line a 20cm (8in) square baking tin with non-stick baking paper.

Melt the butter and malt extract (or molasses or honey) in a saucepan on a medium heat.

Mix the rest of the ingredients together in a large bowl. Add the melted butter and malt and mix well.

Transfer to the lined tin and spread it out in an even layer, pressing down well into all the corners. Bake in the preheated oven for 15 minutes. Allow to cool for 5 minutes, then cut into 12 squares while still warm.

Allow to cool completely on a wire rack, then pop them into an airtight container or biscuit tin so that they maintain their malty chewiness.

CAMPFIRE STEW

SERVES 2 (EASILY DOUBLED)

I make a variation of this all the time, sometimes indoors, sometimes outdoors. You can add eggs if you have them, same with feta, spring onion and fresh herbs. It's adaptable to what you have and what is easiest to transport or keep fresh.

2 tbsp olive oil

1 tbsp garlic powder

1 tbsp smoked paprika

1 tsp chilli flakes or harissa

1 x 400g (14oz) tin of chopped tomatoes

about 250ml (1 cup) water

zest and juice of 1 lemon

1 tbsp light brown sugar

sea salt and cracked black pepper

1 x 400g (14oz) tin of cannellini, kidney or black beans, drained and rinsed

1 x 340g (12oz) tin of sweetcorn

2 eggs (optional)

TO GARNISH (OPTIONAL):

50g (1¾oz) feta cheese

1 spring onion, thinly sliced

a handful of fresh herbs like dill, parsley and/or mint, roughly chopped

Heat the oil in a large saucepan or heavy-based casserole on a medium-low heat. Add the garlic powder, smoked paprika, chilli flakes or harissa and 1–2 tablespoons of the chopped tomatoes. Stir until well combined and allow to sizzle for a couple of minutes. Add the remaining chopped tomatoes, then fill the empty tin halfway with water (this is the 250ml (1 cup) of water called for in the ingredients list) and add that to the pot along with the lemon juice (save the zest for garnish), sugar and some salt and pepper.

Bring to a gentle simmer on a medium heat and allow to bubble away for about 20 minutes. Stir in the beans and sweetcorn, then use a spoon to make two wells in the sauce for the eggs (if using). Gently break an egg into each well, then cover the pot with a lid and cook for 10–12 minutes, until the eggs are cooked through but hopefully still have runny yolks.

If using garnishes, crumble the feta on top, then scatter over the lemon zest, spring onion and fresh herbs.

BLASTA BOOKS #16

LIFE IS SWEET & MESSY

HOW TO FAIL WITH GOOD TASTE

Let me tell you about The Burned Cake.

One of my favourite food projects was the recipe column I had for the *Sunday Times* in 2021. It was such fun to work on the accompanying photographs of the recipes with my friends Cliodhna and Lydia, who were the photographer and food stylist, respectively. We did the shoots for the column at Cliodhna's house, where the kitchen is home to a beautiful Aga, which, it soon became clear, I did not know how to use. At all.

In preparation for our first shoot, I put my coffee cake inside the Aga to bake. When I went to check on it 35 minutes later, I was aghast to discover a molten block of the deepest black that any human eye had ever perceived. I had performed alchemy, for this was no longer a cake. It had chemically, metaphysically, existentially transformed into some kind of meteorite.

Once the shock wore off, the laughter set in. We managed to salvage some of the cake, cutting off its burned casing and uncovering a surprisingly delicious cake underneath. It tasted of coffee and … toast.

One of my favourite flavour combinations is coffee, toast and marmalade, so the next time I made my coffee cake – in a conventional oven that I was familiar with – I added some orange zest and juice, and it changed the recipe for the better.

Many of our most beloved dishes evolved through mistakes. Tarte Tatin. Cornflakes. Worcestershire sauce. Caesar salad. Buffalo wings. If you dig into the history of these iconic ingredients and dishes, you'll discover mistakes, messiness, absent-mindedness or unexpected necessity.

If I was to write a list of my most important lessons in life and what happened in the lead-up to them, I wouldn't be surprised to find that they were the direct consequences of fuckups, both major and minor. I'm actually very successful at failing. It's a key strength of mine.

But I'm not going to pretend that failing is comfortable. Failing feels awful. I think our relationship to failure, and how we process it, is one of the most important relationships in our lives.

Understanding American psychologist Carol Dweck's theory of fixed vs. growth mindset transformed my relationship with mistakes and failure. Dweck argues that people with a fixed mindset believe their talents and abilities are fixed and can't be changed, whereas people with a growth mindset believe their abilities can change through hard work and practice.

You may develop one of these mindsets because of how you are praised – are you praised for your talents or are you praised for how hard you work at your talents? You may have a growth mindset about one part of your life, e.g. cooking, and a fixed mindset about another part of your life, e.g. dating.

Reading Dweck's seminal book *Mindset* was like reading my own painful, fixed mindset-motivated biography. What resonated most with me was the explanation of why failure feels so intolerable to someone with a fixed mindset. If you feel your talents and abilities are fixed, it tends to also mean that you overidentify with and put all your value into these abilities. So when you fail, it's not 'I made a mistake', it feels like 'I *am* a mistake'. With those high stakes, it's no wonder some of us panic when baking a cake.

It sucks to throw away ingredients and start again. You've 'wasted' time and money. And you didn't even get any frickin' cake out of it! I know how frustrating it is. But mistakes, as painful and annoying as they might be, also give you an opportunity to learn. If you never try, you'll never learn, and you can't succeed without trying.

THE RECIPES

Failing is a frustrating but inevitable step in learning how to cook. When thinking of your own journey of learning, the coaching and management tool of the four stages of competence can be a useful way to keep yourself motivated and be your own coach or cheerleader. These four stages can be applied to learning how to drive, learning a language, learning DIY – anything at all.

1. **Unconscious incompetence:** Hey, look at me! I'm baking!
2. **Conscious incompetence:** Oh shit, I don't know what I'm doing. This cake is going to fail. Why did I ever start baking? Help!
3. **Conscious competence:** Hold on, I think this cake is edible. No, wait, it's … delicious! Woohoo, I think I've got this! Let's try again!
4. **Unconscious competence:** I have become one with baking. I don't even measure things or follow recipes anymore. I am the cake and the cake is me. Namaste, etc.

The second stage, conscious incompetence, is where we tend to get stuck, and it's tempting to give up at this stage. Sometimes you can hop between stages two and three in the process of learning. Something that can help you stay motivated is, ironically, the awareness that you're just temporarily incompetent, and that this too shall pass.

I've yet to surpass the conscious competence stage with baking, but honestly, that's good enough for me.

COFFEE & ORANGE CAKE

MAKES 12–16 SLICES

I love this cake because (a) coffee cake is the best, no takebacks, and (b) it's a sweet manifestation of how mistakes can ultimately lead to something even more delicious than you'd originally planned, as I've shared in my story about The Burned Cake on page 58.

You can make your own coffee syrup by reducing coffee and sugar over a simmering heat, but to get that Granny Chic flavour, you're better off using instant coffee (about 1 tablespoon instant coffee to 1 teaspoon of water) or coffee essence.

100g (1 cup) pecans, roughly chopped

225g (½lb) butter, softened

225g (1⅓ cups) dark brown sugar (or light brown or caster)

juice of 1 orange

1–2 tbsp coffee essence

4 eggs

275g (2¼ cups) self-raising flour

2 tsp baking powder

FOR THE ICING:

250g (2 cups) icing sugar

110g (½ cup) butter, softened

3–4 tbsp coffee essence

zest of 1 orange

Preheat the oven to 160°C fan (325°F fan). Line a 30cm x 20cm (12in x 8in) rectangular baking tin with non-stick baking paper.

Spread the pecans out on a baking tray. Toast in the preheated oven for 5 minutes, then allow to cool.

Put the butter and brown sugar in the bowl of a stand mixer fitted with the paddle attachment (or use an electric mixer) and beat together until frothy and smooth. Mix in the orange juice. Don't worry if it splits – when you add the flour, it will come back together. Add 1–2 tablespoons of coffee essence, depending on how strong it is. Whisk in the eggs one at a time. This may split the batter too, but don't worry; once you add the flour to the mix, it will all be okay.

Add half of the toasted, cooled pecans to the batter. Set aside the rest for decorating the cake.

Sieve the flour and baking powder into the bowl. Use a large spoon to fold them in gently.

Pour the batter into the lined cake tin and bake in the preheated oven for 35–40 minutes, until a skewer inserted into the middle of the cake comes out clean. Remove the cake from the oven and allow to cool in the tin for 5 minutes before using the paper to lift it out of the tin onto a wire rack to cool completely.

Meanwhile, make your icing by using your mixer again to beat together the icing sugar, soft butter, 3 tablespoons of coffee essence and the orange zest. Add a bit more icing sugar if the consistency isn't thick enough or a bit more coffee essence to your taste.

Once the cake is cool, put your coffee icing on top and spread it out in a nice even layer. Decorate with the remaining toasted pecans. Cut into slices and serve with a cup of hot coffee.

PINEAPPLE UPSIDE-DOWN CAKE

MAKES 12 SLICES

An upside-down cake is a messy baker's ally. The method of creating a sticky, sugary, buttery glaze comes from a Sara Buenfeld recipe on the BBC Good Food website. The glacé cherries are non-negotiable – 1970s chic, baby.

225g (½lb) butter, cut into chunks and softened, plus extra for greasing

280g (1 1/3 cups) caster sugar

2 tbsp brown sugar

4 medium eggs

2 tsp vanilla extract

350g (3 cups) self-raising flour

2 tsp baking powder

FOR SARA'S TOPPING:

60g (4 tbsp) butter, softened

60g (1/3 cup) light brown sugar

7 pineapple rings tinned in syrup

7 glacé cherries

Preheat the oven to 160°C fan (325°F fan). Grease a 20cm (8in) or 30cm (12in) non-stick round springform cake tin or a square brownie tin with butter, then line it with non-stick baking paper.

To make the topping, beat the butter and brown sugar together until light, creamy and fluffy. Spread this in a thin layer over the base and a quarter of the way up the sides of the round cake tin or just on the bottom of a square brownie tin. Arrange the pineapple rings on top, then pop a glacé cherry in the middle of each pineapple ring. So chic.

To make the cake batter, put the butter and both of the sugars in the bowl of a stand mixer fitted with the paddle attachment (or use an electric mixer or, fair play to you, your own elbow grease) and beat together until light and fluffy. Beat in the eggs one at a time, then add the vanilla. Don't worry if the batter looks curdled at this stage – it will all come together when you add the dry ingredients.

Sieve the flour and baking powder into a large mixing bowl. Add the wet ingredients to the dry and use a wooden spoon or spatula to gradually and gently fold the ingredients together until it all comes together into a batter, being careful not to overmix, as that will result in a heavier cake.

Pour the batter into the tin, covering all the pineapple slices on the bottom. Bake in the preheated oven for 45–55 minutes, until golden brown and a skewer inserted into the middle of the cake comes out clean. Allow to cool in the tin for 10 minutes.

MESSY

Now for the finale! Unclip the cake tin if you've used a springform tin. Put a large chopping board or serving platter on top of the cake. Take a deep breath and turn the cake over onto the board or plate. Peel off the baking paper to reveal the sticky, gooey, caramelised pineapple slices glistening on top of this delicious cake. Exhale.

Allow to cool fully, then cut into 12 slices.

PAULINE'S PAVLOVA

MAKES 12 SLICES

This is the single most precious recipe in this book, for it is my mother's recipe. Sure, a great pavlova is as close to perfect as a pudding can get, but what makes pavlova so special to me is that my mum, Pauline, has made it for me, my family and our special guests for over four decades.

This pavlova has been one of the few constants in my life. It has moved homes and countries with us. It has aged supremely well over the four decades that I have known it, perhaps because it has a special secret ingredient: nostalgia.

As a kid, I loved helping my mum make the pavlova. My payment was not only a generous slice for dessert but getting to lick the mixing bowl. I would watch as she separated the eggs, helping her remove any rogue shells from the egg whites. She'd always give me a go using the electric whisk and show me when the stiff peaks were just stiff enough.

When Mum would thoroughly scrape almost every last speck of meringue off the spoon and mixing bowl, I'd watch in dismay, like, what the hell, lady, those are my WAGES you're scooping out there! But she never forgot to leave a little bit behind in the bowl for me.

Being able to make this pavlova myself keeps me close to Pauline and to the memories of our family being around tables together over the years. Food has that power of connection for me, and I'm grateful for it.

The best version of this pavlova I ever made was when I forgot to set the timer properly and the oven accidentally turned itself off, I'd guess for about the last 15 minutes of the cooking time. I don't know exactly how long, though, so it's been hard for me to replicate that perfection – but that's the joy of cooking. Sometimes, against all odds, it turns out just right.

---

6 eggs, at room temperature

1 tsp distilled white vinegar

200g (1 cup) caster sugar

FOR THE TOPPING:

180ml (¾ cup) double cream

2 kiwis, peeled and sliced

fresh strawberries, blueberries, raspberries or your choice of fresh fruit

---

Preheat your oven to 130°C fan (265°F fan). Cool is key. Line a large baking tray with non-stick baking paper.

Get a large bowl for your egg whites and a smaller bowl for your egg yolks. My mum's top tip here is to separate the eggs into the two bowls one at a time, then use a third spotlessly clean, dry bowl to put each egg white into, one at a time, after you've separated them individually. Doing it this way means you're less likely to get any eggshells or broken yolks in the main egg white mixture. It's important not to get even a speck of yolk in with the whites, otherwise they'll never form stiff peaks (which is also why you need a spotlessly clean, dry bowl). This isn't a time for messiness, as my mum learned the hard way. She says,

MESSY

'Sometimes bits of the yolk can burst and get into the big bowl, so by doing one at a time, you don't end up having to discard what you've done and start again.'

Using an electric whisk, whip the egg whites for a few minutes, until they're pretty dry and start to fluff up a bit. Add your vinegar and whisk for another minute, then gradually add the sugar through a fine mesh sieve and keep mixing until the mixture is beautifully glossy and will stand in soft peaks. I like to think of this mixture as a silky unicorn's mane or fluffy pillow – you want it to stand on its head. This won't take any longer than 5 minutes, so be careful not to overmix.

Pile the meringue onto your lined baking tray, then quickly smooth it out to the shape you want – I love the traditional circle, but a roulade is fun too. Mum says, 'Don't pat it or spread it too long.'

Bake in the preheated oven for 50–55 minutes. FOR THE LOVE OF ALL THAT IS GOOD IN THIS WORLD, DO NOT OPEN THE OVEN DOOR AT THIS STAGE! The urgency and importance of this was drilled into us as kids, so I'm just passing my disproportionately intense fear of ovens opened mid-bake to you now.

After the 50–55 minutes are up, open the oven for a peek. The pavlova should have risen slightly and caramelised around its edges to produce a lightly browned, tantalisingly cracked surface.

When it's ready, remove the tray from the oven and let the pavlova cool a bit before taking a deep breath and inverting it onto a serving plate or dish so that the flat bottom is now facing up. Carefully peel off the baking paper. Even if the pavlova breaks when you flip it over or peel off the paper, you can cover it up with the whipped cream and still have a stunning dessert.

Leave to cool for a few hours. It can stay in the fridge overnight, but Mum and I both like to make it fresh.

Just before serving, whip the cream until it's nice and thick, then spread it all over the top of the pavlova. Decorate with kiwi slices and dry-ish fruit such as strawberries and blueberries, or whatever is in season and will look beautiful.

Serve in big, beautiful slices and marvel at the fluff of your meringue.

INDEX

A
all-rounder roast chicken 28
an easy cheeseboard 48

B
banana: toast with notions 8–9
bars: malty muesli bars 55
beef: slow-cooked beef and harissa stew 40–1
beetroot
    smoked mackerel bites with beetroot dip 38–9
    toast with notions 8–9
biscuits for cheese 47
bread
    caraway brown bread 18
    seedy loaf 19
buttered greens 43

C
cacao: toast with notions 8–9
Caesar salad 23
cake
    coffee and orange cake 60–1
    pineapple upside-down cake 62–3
campfire stew 56
can't cope one-pot pasta 12
caraway brown bread 18
cauliflower: Queen Cauliflower 42
cheese
    an easy cheeseboard 48
    biscuits for cheese 47
    macaroni and cheese 24–5
chicken
    all-rounder roast chicken 28
    homemade chicken stock 29
chocolate: peanut butter and chocolate-dipped dates 54

coconut: spicy coconut noodle soup 33
coffee and orange cake 60–1
cottage cheese: toast with notions 8–9

D
dates: peanut butter and chocolate-dipped dates 54
dip: smoked mackerel bites with beetroot dip 38–9

E
eggs
    eggs, pickles and Marmite 21
    green eggs 22
    messy eggs 6

G
green eggs 22
greens: buttered greens 43

H
harissa: slow-cooked beef and harissa stew 40–1
homemade chicken stock 29
hot chocolate with Tunnock's Tea Cake 13
hummus: toast with notions 8–9

K
kimchi: toast with notions 8–9

L
lemon and orzo soup 30–1

M
macaroni and cheese 24–5
malty muesli bars 55
Marmite: eggs, pickles and Marmite 21
meringues: nonchalant meringues 46

MESSY

messy eggs 6
miso and mushroom broth 32
muesli: malty muesli bars 55
mushrooms: miso and mushroom broth 32

N
nonchalant meringues 46
noodles
    pimped-up instant noodle pot 10
    spicy coconut noodle soup 33

O
orange: coffee and orange cake 60–1
orzo: lemon and orzo soup 30–1

P
pasta
    can't cope one-pot pasta 12
    macaroni and cheese 24–5
pavlova: Pauline's pavlova 64–5
peanut butter
    peanut butter and chocolate-dipped dates 54
    toast with notions 8–9
pickles: eggs, pickles and Marmite 21
pimped-up instant noodle pot 10
pineapple upside-down cake 62–3
potatoes: smushed spuds 45

Q
Queen Cauliflower 42

S
salad: Caesar salad 23
seedy loaf 19
slow-cooked beef and harissa stew 40–1
smoked mackerel bites with beetroot dip 38–9
smushed spuds 45

soup
    lemon and orzo soup 30–1
    miso and mushroom broth 32
    spicy coconut noodle soup 33
spicy coconut noodle soup 33
stew
    campfire stew 56
    slow-cooked beef and harissa stew 40–1
stock
    homemade chicken stock 29
    vegetable stock 29

T
tahini sauce 44
toast with notions 8–9
Tunnock's Tea Cake, with hot chocolate 13

V
vegetable stock 29

Nine Bean Rows
23 Mountjoy Square
Dublin, D01 E0F8
Ireland
@9beanrowsbooks
ninebeanrowsbooks.com

Blasta Books is an imprint of Nine Bean Rows Books Ltd.
@blastabooks blastabooks.com

First published 2025
Text copyright © Aoife McElwain, 2025
Illustrations copyright © Ciara Coogan, 2025

ISBN: 978-1-7384795-9-7

Editor: Kristin Jensen
Series artist: Ciara Coogan
cicoillustrates.com
Designer: Jane Matthews
janematthews.ie
Proofreader: Jocelyn Doyle
Printed by L&C Printing Group, Poland

This product is made of material from well-managed, FSC®-certified forests and other controlled sources.

All rights reserved.

No part of this publication may be copied, reproduced or transmitted in any form or by any means without written permission of the publishers.

A CIP catalogue record for this book is available from the British Library.

For EU product safety concerns, contact us at info@ninebeanrowsbooks.com.

10 9 8 7 6 5 4 3 2 1

About the author

Aoife McElwain is a messy cook who lives with her girlfriend Anstice in Connemara, in the West of Ireland, where the wild beauty of the landscape helps balance her work as a food writer, food stylist, wedding DJ, events planner, creativity coach, earnest barista and aspiring cheesemaker.

Aoife is Chief Craic Mechanic at Sing Along Social, a singing party for people who can't sing, and pops up at weddings and festivals in Ireland, Europe, the US or wherever the craic calls. In the summertime, she's a rather clumsy but endlessly enthusiastic waitress at Little Fish, a family-run restaurant in Cleggan, Co. Galway.

She started a food blog in 2009 to learn how to cook and wrote a weekly food column for *Sunday Times Ireland* in 2021. Her words about food have also been featured in the *Irish Times*, *Irish Independent*, *Totally Dublin Magazine*, *Financial Times* and the *Guardian*. She published a book about burnout, *Slow at Work*, in 2018.

In her free time, Aoife volunteers on a beautiful hillside sheep farm and with Connemara Ponies. She finds spending time with animals and in nature to be a therapeutic balm for her busy, messy brain.

@aoifemcelwain